"Most everyone will agree that customer satisfaction is important. But how many of us truly know how to measure our customers' satisfaction accurately and precisely? In *Managing Forward*, Larry Freed shows us how to understand our customers' experience in a scientific, quantifiable manner that allows us to predict their future interactions with us. It's pure gold!"

—Kevin Ertell, CMO, OnlineShoes.com

"Larry Freed and ForeSee have made an immeasurable and positive difference in the quality of federal agency websites. Larry Freed has a gift for distilling the essential drivers of improvement and driving us to action. Executives take note—if you are serious about improving customer service on your website, you must use ForeSee analytics."

—Tina Sung, Vice President, Partnership for Public Service

"*Managing Forward* is a remarkably useful and easy-to-read tutorial on the importance of metrics in today's age of the digital consumer. It's a 'must read' for every marketing professional on how to measure consumer behavior today and translate those measurements into happier customers and better business tomorrow. Larry Freed brings the old adage 'You are what you measure' up-to-date with his excellent exposition on the power of metrics."

—Tom Porter, Executive-in-Residence, Zell Lurie Institute for Entrepreneurial Studies at the University of Michigan

"No business survives without satisfied customers...a simple concept business leaders often fail to embrace. Foresee Results is a must-consider solution."

—Michael Finney, President and CEO of the Michigan Economic Development Corporation

"This is a highly understandable view of a critically important issue to all businesses—how to better understand their customers and use that understanding to drive profitable sales growth. After many years of focusing on supply chain optimization, it is now time to focus on demand growth. This terrific book provides an actionable 'how to' guide to improve measurable customer understanding quickly and with minimal cost. A must read for any business leader looking to improve sales."

—Joyce Hrinya, CEO A&R Strategy Partners, LLC

"Larry Freed is one of the leading figures in customer experience analytics today. His work on measuring satisfaction is a must read for any business executive."

—Richard Wolff, COO, Javelin Group

## Advance Praise for *Managing Forward*

"You can't manage what you can't measure" the saying goes. Yet all t often we don't measure what matters or fail to create actionable insigl from the streams of data filling our dashboards every day. Larry Fre knows what matters and knows how to measure it. His book *Managi Forward* is a fascinating unveiling of the simple truths behind the s ence of customer satisfaction and its power to predict future behavi How does he know? He asked! Larry has taken a lifetime of knowled devoted to understanding and measuring customer satisfaction from engineer's steel-eyed perspective and explains it in easy to use and e; to implement terms. *Managing Forward* is a marketer's must-read."

—Bruce Rogers, Chief Insight Officer, Forbes Me

"Websites provide companies with tons of data they never had bef about customer behavior, but surprisingly little insight on how to expa a business by satisfying customers. The techniques presented in *Man. ing Forward* help web and corporate managers decipher what all tl data is telling them about what the customer really wants. Larry Free one of the country's top experts when it comes to measuring custor satisfaction. In the Internet age, customers truly possess the power kings. This is a book that allows management to read the king's mind

—Jack Love, Publisher of *Internet Retailer*
Author of *McDonalds: Behind the Arc*

"Larry Freed and Foresee are at the forefront of helping organizatic understand the importance of customer satisfaction."

—Hal Lawton, President, Home Depot On

"Larry Freed and Customer Satisfaction are synonyms in the minds nearly everyone who works professionally on the Internet. His evangel for the American Customer Satisfaction Index is only shadowed by efforts to ensure that ForeSee Results customers deliver great experien online. *Managing Forward* is the next logical extension of Larry's w to create a better, more useful, and more satisfying internet, and undoubtedly be considered a 'must read' for business leaders workin( this increasingly digital world."

—Eric T. Peterson, Author, *Web Analytics Demysti*

"Larry Freed opened my eyes about measuring the success of online n keting vis-à-vis customer satisfaction. It wasn't just his deep knowled but his uncanny talent at explaining how customer opinion transl; into bottom line results. His avuncular approach comes through loud ; clear in *Managing Forward* making it a joy to read."

—Jim Sterne, Founder, eMetrics Marketing Optimiza·
Summit and Chairman, Web Analytics Associat

# MANAGING FORWARD

## How to Move from Measuring the Past to Managing the Future

### By Larry Freed

with a chapter by
**Claes Fornell**
author of *The Satisfied Customer*

ISBN-10: 0-6155276-0-4
ISBN-13: 978-806155276-0-4

**ForeSee**
Corporate Headquarters
2500 Green Road
Suite 400
Ann Arbor, MI 48105
www.foresee.com

**ForeSee UK**
1 Northumberland Avenue
Trafalgar Square
London, WC2N 5BW
United Kingdom

Book design and composition by Rick Soldin, Kingsport, TN
Printed and bound in the United States of America

# CONTENTS

# ACKNOWLEDGEMENTS

There are many people to acknowledge and thank. Without their help, support, inspiration, and knowledge this book would not exist.

It starts with family. Growing a business is more than a full-time job. Without the support provided by my wife Laini and my sons Josh, Danny and Jake, none of this would be possible. Their understanding of the many business trips and late work nights and constant support and encouragement make it all possible. There are not enough words to describe my appreciation.

Along the way you meet many people that influence your approach, teach you important lessons, and help you develop and mature in the business world. While there are too many to list, a few rise to the top, and I thank them for all they have taught me. Dr. Claes Fornell opened my eyes to the importance of the customer and the power of being able to measure customer satisfaction. The support and guidance from the rest of the ForeSee Board (Barry Goldsmith, Noah Walley, Phil Dur, Conor Mullet) has been critical as we continue to grow and expand. Dave Schott, my first manager, taught me about the importance of hard work. I learned many important lessons from Peter Karmanos about growing and scaling a business.

And the many entrepreneurs and CEOs I have had the privilege to know have provided countless insights that helped evolve my knowledge.

Without the team from ForeSee there would be no ForeSee and no book. To steal a line from Bo Schembechler, one of the greatest football coaches of all time: "The Team, The Team, The Team." It is the team that wins, not the individuals, both in sports and in business. There are too many to list but every individual has contributed both to my individual growth and the growth and success of ForeSee.

I'd also like to thank our clients, who I consider to be some of my greatest teachers and a true extension of our ForeSee team. Our business succeeds because of our passionate, loyal clients, and not a day passes that I don't learn something new or look at something in a new way because of a client.

Without Sarah Allen-Short's hard work, great insights, pushing, nagging and encouragement this book would only be an idea. And Jeff Haden's literary excellence helped bring it all together.

My acknowledgements started with family and ends with family. I learned many lessons from my father, Jack, that are central to my approach to business and to life. The wisdom he had, learned and honed over many years of owning and growing a business, cannot be found in business books or MBA classes—and while I have not mastered it all, every bit I learned is irreplaceable. While he unfortunately is no longer alive, I hope that in some way I carry on his wisdom and can pass some of my father's legacy along to my sons.

# INTRODUCTION

**W**orst case scenario? Even if our meeting turned out to be a bust, I would at least enjoy a great lunch at Zingerman's Deli, one of my favorite restaurants since my undergraduate days at the University of Michigan.

As the Vice President of E-Business at Compuware, the IT colossus that today serves nearly all of the largest Fortune 500 companies, one of the more fun parts of my job was helping to evaluate and explore partnerships, joint ventures, and acquisitions related to the fast-emerging "e" world. It was the year 2000, and we had survived the transition into the new millennium with hardly any problems. Focusing on the Internet was exciting, a prospect filled with endless ideas and opportunities.

Sometimes those explorations turned out to be dead ends or not particularly good fits for Compuware, but occasionally there was something of interest. So as I drove from Compuware's headquarters to Ann Arbor to meet Claes Fornell, Professor of Business at the Stephen M. Ross School of Business at the University of Michigan and the creator of the American Customer Satisfaction Index (ACSI), I knew I would at least meet an incredibly smart guy with an interesting idea about building a new customer satisfaction-based business.

However, I wasn't sure it would be a particularly useful idea, at least where Compuware was concerned.

Don't get me wrong. Even then I believed in the concept of customer satisfaction. No business survives without satisfied customers. I got that. But prior to joining Compuware, my experience at various financial institutions, including as Chief Technology Officer for Bank One, left me with the impression that customer satisfaction efforts tended to end up like other initiatives such as TQM (Total Quality Management), Five 9s (reliability to 99.999%), Zero Defects (striving for no quality defects), BPR (Business Process Reengineering), and even Six Sigma (Motorola-developed strategy utilizing quality methods and statistical analysis). Many programs sound great, look great, get people excited, and sometimes even add a little value, but very rarely can you quantify the impact on a company's bottom line. The average satisfaction program went the way of the dinosaur after a few months.

Similarly, traditional satisfaction studies I had seen in the past were short-lived and ineffective. Data and action plans were shared in follow-up meetings and quickly forgotten as we filed away the fancy, chart-filled binders and went back to actually running the business. A few months later the new flavor-of-the-month comes along, complete with more meetings and more binders.

Every smart company and every smart manager knows that customer satisfaction always has been and should be a business goal. But without the value of a concrete metric you can actually use to manage a business and quantify tangible results, customer satisfaction efforts were, in my experience, non-specific and lacking in meaning and direction.

So with large grains of salt at the ready and visions of a Zingerman's Reuben sandwich dancing in my head, I sat down to meet with Claes that morning. To say I was immediately blown away and my life was instantly changed might make this sound more like a self-help book than a business book, but that is exactly what happened.

I was aware of but largely unfamiliar with the American Customer Satisfaction Index (ACSI) that Claes and his colleagues at the University of Michigan had created. I saw the results published in the *Wall Street Journal* every quarter, and I knew the ACSI was a macroeconomic indicator economists used to predict Gross Domestic Product and consumer spending. I also knew the ACSI released customer satisfaction scores for hundreds of individual companies each year, but I didn't really know what those numbers meant or what the companies did with them.

During our very first conversation on that day in 2000, Claes erased my vague notions of customer satisfaction as a nice, warm, fuzzy program with little to no actual value or actionable, predictive ability as a metric.

Claes showed me how, when measured correctly using a scientific approach, customer satisfaction could actually predict the future of a business and help companies decide where to focus their improvement efforts in order to optimize their investments and maximize their returns. As Claes describes in his chapter on the ACSI (Chapter 6), he had created a methodology that could:

> Measure what we can't see with our own eyes (e.g. customer attitudes and expectations)

> Put non-observables into a cause-and-effect system (the ACSI statistical engine)

> Separate the relevant from the trivial (smart companies need to know the difference between what people complain about loudest and what actually

impacts their likely future behaviors, which are often very different things)

> Generalize from a small sample to a target population (a methodology that allows for a smaller sample size while still maintaining statistical significance at a high confidence interval, saving companies millions of dollars)

> Use the customer experience to accurately and reliably predict financial success and other desired outcomes

Claes had the methodology in place and years of research behind it. Hundreds of companies around the world had already used the methodology in various forms to manage their businesses. On that day in 2000, Claes talked about developing a very specific technology based on the ACSI methodology and then applying that technology to websites, since the web provided such a natural, popular, and inexpensive way to collect data. Customer satisfaction data that had previously cost millions to collect could be collected online for a fraction of the cost. A standardized technology based on his methodology would allow managers and executives to connect customer experience to the bottom line and to confidently optimize the efforts that will achieve desired business objectives.

Suddenly, I saw customer satisfaction not as a warm and fuzzy program worthy of a few inspirational posters in a lobby but as an incredibly robust and powerful management tool. My underlying reservations about customer satisfaction "programs" had not changed; what I now saw was not a program but an actionable metric. What I now had was a way to objectively quantify the direct impact of satisfied customers on a company's bottom line.

Even so, this is not a book about how I met Claes or about what ForeSee can do. This is a book about a fundamental business problem that excellent customer satisfaction management can help address.

Most companies focus on what has happened in the past to determine the strategies and tactics that should drive their futures. They look at how much they sold last month or last year, how many visitors they had, what their profit margin was, how last year's advertising program worked, etc. Then they decide what should happen next by looking at metrics that describe what already occurred.

The old cliché "you can't drive forward when you're looking in the rear-view mirror" really does describe a fundamental management issue at play in most companies around the world. That perspective is understandable; most of the things we measure are chosen because they are easy to count, not because they are business-critical metrics that measure success now and in the future.

Customer satisfaction, on the other hand, can actually predict the future when measured correctly, since extensive scientific and academic research shows a satisfied customer is a long-term, loyal, and profitable customer who is likely to recommend you to others –future customer behaviors are absolutely critical to the success of any business.

If you know your customer satisfaction score and you know how to increase your score, you can then increase sales, return visits, recommendations, loyalty, and brand engagement across all channels.

Fundamentally, I think great businesses achieve great success when great people make great decisions. But "the great people" theory is only one piece of the management and corporate leadership puzzle. Better, more reliable, and more useful data leads to better decisions and better results.

Think about a business decision you made that did not turn out particularly well and that, in hindsight, you feel was a mistake. I am willing to bet your mistake was not based on a lack of effort, a lack of intelligence, a lack of good intentions, or even a lack of data. Your mistake was almost certainly the result of incorrect or insufficient data or the result of an inability to turn correct and precise data into an actionable strategy moving forward. We all try to do the right things, but sometimes doing the right things is hard when you don't have the information you need.

Thinking, feeling, and having opinions are not enough, no matter how great the leader. Managing effectively is based on turning data into information and information into intelligence.

After meeting with Claes I went back to Compuware and sat down with Scott Johnson. Scott was working on the corporate development team at the time. We developed an organizational and financial model for a business, created a solid business plan, and delivered it to Pete Karmanos, the Compuware CEO. He liked the idea and wanted to get it started...so much so that a few weeks later asked me to leave Compuware and run the new company.

I have to admit I hesitated. Joining a new company, even a company spun off from my employer, represented a personal and professional risk. I loved my job at Compuware, and starting any new business, no matter how much time I was able to spend analyzing and evaluating the opportunity, naturally involves some amount of risk.

However, two major factors made me know we could be successful:

1. I knew the ACSI methodology gave us a sustainable competitive advantage.

**2.** I realized emerging web technology could streamline the process and open up an entirely new market sector.

Moreover, the key stakeholders were positive, nurturing, and supportive, which I realize in retrospect was actually a third factor that played a major role in ForeSee's immediate and continued success. In truth, pairing Claes Fornell (a brilliant academic who had developed a genius methodology inspired by watching submarines in his native Sweden) with Pete Karmanos (a successful entrepreneur who in 1975 used a tax refund check to build a multi-billion dollar public technology company with two colleagues) could have been a disaster in the making. Claes and Pete were very different people with very different strengths.

Yet both of these men had an important trait in common. They knew what they knew, they knew what they *didn't* know, and they each held great respect for the other's expertise. I have met too many people in my career who assume success and expertise in one area makes them an expert in every area, an assumption that rarely turns out to be accurate. Claes and Pete, both exceptional and successful in their own fields, understood and valued what the other person brought to the table. I knew this was a set of stakeholders with qualities that would ensure our success.

Since I also am well aware (sometimes painfully so) of all the things I don't know, we chose a small, handpicked group of people to round out our expertise and capabilities as a start-up. Many of those founding employees are still with the company ten years later (as are many of our first clients).

I can't say the process was without challenges, though. One of our first potential clients was the *Detroit Free Press*. At the time they were using a system provided by another company—clumsy and rudimentary, but still competitive to our new technology—to measure customer satisfaction. The *Free Press* agreed to let us implement our methodology so they could see how the two products compared side by side. Unfortunately, before we could put our system in place the competition went out of business.

Watching what we expected to be our biggest competitor close its doors before we launched created, to say the least, major concerns about the state of the marketplace we planned to enter with all our chips on the table. We decided not to bury our heads in the sand but to instead dig deeper and find out why our competition went out of business. After fairly intensive research we had the information we needed to forge ahead, smarter and stronger, armed with a plan to succeed where our competition had failed.

I see it this way. Within every failure there is a tremendous amount to learn. You often hear successful entrepreneurs say we should not be afraid to fail, that we should learn from our failures, that we should jump right into the fray. While I partly agree with that viewpoint, the better option is to not fail at all—and to learn from the failure of others, as we were lucky enough to do. Anyone who knows me knows that I *hate* losing, and in my mind, failure is not and has never been an option.

Still, I can't say our timing was perfect. We went to beta one week after September 11, 2001. The economy tumbled and companies stopped spending on capital projects, so we took a step back and revised our growth forecasts.

Yet we also forged ahead, confident in our ability to serve a real need. What started out in 2001 as a scientific, robust, incredibly sophisticated technology used to measure online customer satisfaction continues to expand: deeper into the online customer experience analytics and broader into other channels of customer satisfaction analytics (like call centers, stores, banking centers, mobile sites and apps, kiosks, iPads, social media channels, etc.)

Claes and I never made it to Zingerman's that day. For the first time in my life, I didn't mind missing out on their famous Reuben sandwich.

Instead, I took my first steps toward moving from measuring the past to managing the future, both for my own growing company and for the hundreds of companies that have come to rely on our technology.

Ten years into our adventure seems like a good time to take a step back and share some of what we have learned along the way, including how companies get it right, how they get it wrong, and how our customers and their experiences are the most powerful, forward-looking management tool we have.

Larry Freed
*Ann Arbor, Michigan*

# chapter 1

# KNOW WHAT YOU DON'T KNOW

In some ways the web is the most important customer touch point where data, measurement tools, and analytics are concerned. Collecting data online is easy and inexpensive relative to other channels. We can measure actions on the web that are very difficult and costly to measure in other channels. For those reasons, and because the web is where we got our start as a company, this book will focus on web measurement but the broader concepts apply to all businesses in all industries across all consumer touch points. Today ForeSee applies these concepts and technologies to all touch points across many companies.

Most websites not only provide a channel of interaction but also form a part of the multichannel experience consumers have with your business. The web can serve as a research tool for a customer planning to buy from a retail store, a support tool for the customer of a product manufacturer, an information tool for a consumer packaged goods company or pharmaceutical customer, a resource tool for patients of a hospital, an alternative for a viewer who watches shows on both television and on the web...and the list goes on. This makes the web far and away the best place to comprehensively collect a wide variety of data in order to measure not only the web customer experience but also the customer experience across all channels.

## Buried in Data

As a result of the data collection capabilities inherent on the Internet, the web is also the easiest place to become buried in data. Many valuable analytical tools are easy to implement and produce reams of data. But what do you do with all the data you generate? If you are a manager or executive you may not see all the detail, but trust me—the detail is there (and if it's not you have a different problem.)

Most managers and executives (myself included) do not always know what to do with all that data or, more importantly, how to act on that data.

The right tools and analysis can turn data into information, information into intelligence, and intelligence into action. With actionable intelligence you will understand your visitors, whether they are actual customers or only browsers. With intelligence, you will make smarter decisions, not only in strategic terms but in tactical terms as well.

Intelligence lets you make smarter decisions in all channels: from web to mobile, from call centers to in-store shopping, wherever you serve your customers. But "actionable intelligence" sounds like vague, jargon business-speak. What do I actually mean by "intelligence?" I promise to be very specific as we move through this book.

# What You Know

Think about the measurement tools you have in place and the metrics you use to track your performance over a broad spectrum of activities. In terms of customer behavior you most likely know a lot about your customers, potentially including (depending on your industry and channel):

> How visitors came to your site

> Which pages visitors clicked

> What information or products visitors looked for

> How long visitors stayed (in terms of page views and overall time spent on the site)

> Where and when visitors left your site

> What visitors purchased and what they abandoned

> How many calls your call center received

> How long callers waited on hold

> What percentage of calls were resolved on the first call

> How many consumers entered your store

> What percentage of shoppers purchased in your store

> Your average order size

> Your customer renewal rate

> Your customer acquisition costs

> And so on...

Internal analysts, and in some cases outside vendors, help collect, manage, tabulate, and sort all this data into report after report detailing how performance has changed over time. Most organizations have robust system of metrics and key performance indicators (KPIs) in place to make some sense of the data generated, typically using metrics like bounce rate and conversion rate.

In fact, so many behavioral metrics and KPIs exist that excellent books have been written on the subject (including a personal favorite of mine, Eric Peterson's *The Big Book of Key Performance Indicators*.) The Web Analytics Association also published a 34-page document filled with web analytics definitions.

Traditional web analytics produce data. Data allows you to know a lot about your business and about your customers. We definitely need to know how many visitors we had, how long it takes a page to load, how much we sold last year, and how long people spent on a site. Data is important. Data is critical. Data is absolutely vital. I use data to understand what happened in our own business yesterday, last week, last month, and last year—and I expect our managers to do the same.

But that's just it. The crux of the issue is that data looks *backward*. Data tells you what already happened, not what will happen next or how to *influence* what will happen next.

Once the metrics are calculated, the pie charts created, and the dashboards distributed, what have you learned? What information has been generated that you can act upon with confidence? I struggle with this in our own business. What intelligence have I gained as a result of all the data I have about our business, and more importantly, what will I do about it?

Like you, I know a lot about our business. But when you use data alone there is a lot you don't know, and what you do not know could critically impact the future of your business.

# What You May Not Know Can Hurt You

The key is to know what you know—and to know what you *don't* know. This is a key principle I stress over and over to our staff. Due to the volume and breadth of data generated by analytics tools, it is easy to assume you know a lot more about your site visitors than you could ever possibly need to know or act on. There are probably times you wish you had less data. You do know a lot about what your visitors did—but there is also likely to be a lot you do not know.

Think about your current measurement tools, and the data you possess and use in various reports and dashboards. (Most of the following examples apply to websites but have parallels in the offline world as well.)

Do you know:

> Why visitors come to your site (to research, to buy, to complete a transaction, to get product support, to learn more about your company before interacting with you through another touch point, etc.)?

> What influences visits to your site (a referral, a social media interaction, a failure to resolve an issue with a call center, an advertisement, a news story, a previous affinity with your brand, etc.) and which customer acquisition sources result in traffic that is the mostly likely to convert?

> What visitors need from your website? How needs differ by population segment or other segmentation that is useful to your business—perhaps first-time vs. repeat visitors, heavy users vs. light users, etc.?

> What visitors expect from your website? Do men and women have the same expectations? Old and young? Do people who arrived as a result of a Google ad have the same expectations as those who arrived because of a TV ad?

> What channel your visitors prefer, and are there ways you can influence that preference so they frequent less costly, more profitable channels?

> How customers view your business, compared to the way non-customers view your business, relative to your competition?

> How your customer profiles and expectations change in response to market and broader economic conditions? And what, if anything, you need to change as a result?

> How the online experience of visitors to your site impacts their relationship with your company—across all channels?

> If you do not sell on your website, how you can quantify to company leadership the cross-channel value of your online initiatives, in real and tangible ways?

> Where you should focus your efforts (in terms of targeted tactical enhancements and/or broader strategic plans) to improve the online and offline experience to better achieve overall company goals?

> Where and how you can cut costs and improve operations through greater use of the online channel for customer service and support?

> > The level of satisfaction of your visitors, and how that impacts their future behaviors?

> > What visitors are likely to do after their site visit? Are they likely to recommend you? Buy from you again? Sign up for your newsletter? Download your mobile app? Register for your loyalty program?

That is a lot of questions, and some may apply to your industry. But if you cannot answer most of these questions with confidence (and you can't if you only use behavioral data) you could be missing huge pieces of the puzzle.

I recognize the above list is also relatively broad, albeit with far-reaching consequences and implications that could totally transform a business if properly understood and acted on. Let's drill down to more concrete examples.

| **What You Know...** | **What You May Not Know...** |
| --- | --- |
| People visited an average of 6 pages on your site and stayed for 1 minute and 30 seconds. | How, specifically, can you improve self-service options online in order to deflect and reduce call center traffic and save millions in operating costs while creating a more satisfying experience for customers? |
| 46% of your site visitors abandoned a shopping cart without making a purchase. | How many of those visitors went on to purchase from you through another channel (conversion success) and how many bought from a competitor (conversion failure)? |
| After your last Google ad, you received 17,500 click-throughs. | Did those who clicked through make a purchase? Is one customer acquisition source resulting in better-quality traffic than another? |
| People constantly complain about your prices. | Is that true all year, or just seasonally? Is it true for all customers or only certain segments? Can you develop strategies that take into account actual (instead of assumed) sensitivity to maximize profit? |

| What You Know... | What You May Not Know... |
|---|---|
| You have 23,500 Facebook fans and 17,000 Twitter followers. | How much do those Facebook fans and Twitter followers spend with you? Do your returns, in terms of bottom-line impact, justify your investment in social media? Should you be doing more, or less? |
| You have limited resources (in terms of dollars and people). | Where can you focus limited resources to get the best bang for your buck? Which changes/improvements/enhancements will have the greatest impact on your bottom line? |

Changes in technology and customer behavior make the web channel a crucial element in the success of your entire organization. Using the intelligence that results from having the right measurement tools in place, your organization can focus on developing the right strategies and initiatives that will have the greatest impact.

We'll get to that part, I promise.

First, let's look at your customers and how they have dramatically—and permanently—changed.

# chapter 2

# ACCELERATED DARWINISM

To understand why customer satisfaction is so critical, take a close look at today's consumer.

Years ago the average consumer was like Hamlet, often only allowed to make a single choice. To buy or not to buy, that was the question. Small-town retailers enjoyed a near-monopoly. Need clothes? Pile the family in the car and head to the local department store. Need tools? Off you go to the hardware store around the corner. Need a new TV? Choose from the small selection available at your local retailer. If you needed advice before you made a purchase you depended on local salespeople to provide you with that information.

A similar lack of choices existed across other industries as well. When I was growing up we had three network TV channels to choose from instead of the hundreds of channels available on cable systems today (not to mention Netflix and Hulu and other streaming services.) For news, Detroit had two newspapers to choose from instead of websites updated with breaking news throughout the day, and hundreds of online editions of print newspapers from cities all over the world. My banking choices were limited to those with branches in my neighborhood. And when my parents wanted to book a vacation they went to our local travel agent.

In short, one way or another the business had almost all of the power. When consumers walked through the door they became nearly captive customers. The businesses had the perennial real estate advantage (location, location, location) as well as a definite leg up in terms of information about products, services, and competitors.

Not anymore.

Today most of those near-monopolistic or oligopolistic situations have disappeared. The balance of power—especially the balance of power in terms of information and choice –has dramatically shifted over time towards the consumer.

The result of this shift towards consumer power is a phenomenon I call Accelerated Darwinism, a survival of the business fittest at warp speed.

Accelerated Darwinism is the result of a number of factors, but the communications revolution is by far the most important reason behind the rapid pace of change and the shift in the balance of power between the consumer and business. The consumer appears to be the major beneficiary of this sea change, but I use the word "appears" on purpose. Businesses can also benefit tremendously from not just understanding but also from embracing Accelerated Darwinism.

# The Rise of the Super Consumer

Today's consumers have amazing, superhero-like capabilities. They can:

> Clone themselves by shopping in five stores at once through the use of multi-tabbed browsing or by utilizing multiple channels (shopping in a store while using an iPhone to browse other retailers).

> Speak with an incredibly loud voice by posting on Facebook and Twitter about their experiences—good or bad—with any company.

> Listen to millions of voices via social media rants and recommendations, and listen to friends' opinions on Facebook, Twitter, and email.

> Have as much or even more knowledge than your employees by utilizing the web for customer-generated product reviews, detail specifications, and to scour the competitive landscape.

Even better—for the consumer, at least—they can accomplish all this and more at the same time.

Because the customer's voice is incredibly loud and because so many people can hear it, the impact of customer satisfaction—even at the individual level—is magnified by a factor of thousands and cannot be ignored.

Yesterday's TV shopper walked through a single store, glanced at a few different models, possibly asked a salesperson for help, and made a decision. Today's shopper may do a little research online, cruise the aisles of one or more stores to look at products in person, check online reviews with her iPhone, and then visit an online retailer to complete her shopping...all the while comfortable and secure in the knowledge that if *this* website doesn't have what she needs, she can sprint off to dozens of other online retailers with a few clicks. And regardless of whether her shopping experience is great or terrible, she is likely to tell others on Facebook or Twitter.

Think of today's customer as a world-class sprinter with a megaphone for a mouth and elephant-sized ears. In essence, today's empowered consumer has evolved into the Super Consumer—or in web terms, Customer 2.0.

It is impossible for anyone to predict the new communication tools currently under development, much less which of those tools will capture popular imagination and be adopted by millions of users. What we can guarantee is that any new tools will be broader and faster than the tools we use today. As a result, Super Consumers will share ideas and opinions with more people at a faster speed, and they will also listen to the opinions of many more people at a faster speed. We call this magnified voice of customer.

The Super Consumer will only become more and more powerful over time—not less.

Smart companies already take advantage of the communication revolution. Customers can market on your behalf, and in a much more powerful way. If customers are satisfied they communicate positively; if they are unhappy they communicate negatively. Digital communication and social media have magnified "over the fence" word of mouth exponentially, and there is no turning back.

## Social Media and Magnified Voice of Customer

Voice of customer metrics are based on leveraging an established methodology to identify opportunities that will positively impact customer satisfaction. Accurately gathering voice of customer data involves much more than fielding customer complaints, receiving emails from customers, providing an opportunity for customers to provide feedback, or running an occasional survey; the key is to blend quantitative and qualitative data in a reliable and statistically valid way. Applying science to voice of customer transforms what was a feedback mechanism into a measurement device.

Social Media (Facebook, Google+, Twitter, blogs, etc.) provide another avenue to listen to customer feedback, and because so many people can see it or read it, we call that magnified voice of customer. We can listen, learn, and in some cases respond to the voice of customer feedback from social media. But we need to remember that this information is customer feedback, not measurement.

Hype and "expert" guidance aside, keep in mind that focusing on social media as a customer listening tool to the exclusion of other initiatives could put your business at a long-term competitive disadvantage. If social media is the only place you listen to your customers, you will only listen to a fraction of your customers, and most likely not a representative set. Even with the incredible growth of Facebook and Twitter, many of your customers will not provide feedback on social networks.

Communication tools and techniques will continue to evolve; what will *never* change is the need to listen to the customer. And listen to them everywhere you can. How consumers speak and how you listen to what they say will evolve; our need to listen and as a result be able to predict the future will never change.

# The Balance of Power Has Shifted—Forever

What changes have resulted from the rise of Super Consumer? The balance of "power" in the company/consumer relationship has shifted:

**Increased customer knowledge.** Most customers know a lot more about *you*—and your products and services—than you even begin to know about *them*. They learn by leveraging the Internet to research your products and services and hear what others say about you. While you are fighting off ever-increasing competition, your customers spend their time becoming incredibly educated consumers and using the communication tools at their disposal to spread the word about what they learn.

**Dramatically lower customer switching costs.** Years ago changing from one store to another could be somewhat inconvenient, especially if you had to drive farther. To take your business from one bank to another was also a time consuming hassle. Your ability to switch from one newspaper to another or to switch from one television channel to another was limited to the local choices available.

Today customers can take advantage of a wide variety of communication and buying channels. Don't like your local store? No problem; buy online. Don't like the service of one online retailer? No problem; dozens of other online retailers sell the products you need. Can't get the product information you need? Search the Internet for other sources. Don't like your local newspaper? Go online and have your choice of content from all over the world. Don't like your stockbroker? Open an online brokerage account anywhere.

Fail to satisfy customers and one click of the mouse later they are gone—most likely forever. The customer's cost to switch has dropped like a rock and is often near zero. At little to no switching cost your site visitors and customers will leave you faster than you can spell the word "loyalty." Plus, with the growth in use of smart phones those alternatives are more convenient than ever.

**The barriers to entry are incredibly low.** Super Consumers exist in media, retail, entertainment, B2B, and even in the public and non-profit sectors. When everyone can provide the same commodities, services, and products, how do you compete? Thanks to the Internet and FedEx, every supplier is a global supplier. Thanks to blogs and wikis, every web surfer is a content contributor. Thanks to cell phones with cameras, everyone over the age of five is a photographer.

Customers will use the channel that provides the best experience and best meets their needs and expectations, whether as product/service consumers, information consumers, or content creators.

**Increased competition.** More businesses exist and can compete on a variety of vertical and horizontal levels. The three powerful words that once served to differentiate many businesses—location, location, location—are often now an ineffective business strategy. Add the relatively low cost of running a basic online marketing campaign, of acquiring new customers, of accessing efficient distribution systems, and of establishing granular pricing schemes, and almost anyone can compete with you...plus thanks to low barriers to entry they can probably start competing with you as early as tomorrow and from anywhere in the world—including from your neighbor's basement.

**Single Channel? Multichannel.** Web 2.0 has led to a massive reduction in single-channel consumers. Most consumers no longer get news from a single channel. They watch TV, listen to the radio, read papers, surf the web, follow news on Twitter and use their Kindle and iPad to stay current.

Most consumers do not shop and purchase only in stores. They browse in one channel and purchase in another. They use mobile apps to compare prices. They buy on websites, in stores, and on phones.

Your customers have advantages over you they have never had before. Smart organizations recognize the balance of power has shifted forever. But believe it or not, the power shift does not have to be a bad thing, although it certainly can be. It all comes down to how you handle it.

# From Zero to Billions . . . and Back

The customer has the ultimate power, spurring what I call the Accelerated Darwinism effect: Survival of the fittest and failure of the less then fit, faster then we have ever seen before, due largely to the evolution of the Super Consumer.

Years ago it took decades to build a billion-dollar company. Today companies go from zero to billions and back to zero in a matter of years. Remember Pets.com? As one of the dot-com bubble's most famous "pops," they saw $300 million in venture capital disappear in the space of a few short years. Startups. com, GeoCities.com, Webvan.com, and Freeinternet.com met similar fates along with dozens of other businesses made and broken in a few short years.

On the flip side, Newegg.com, an online retailer of computer hardware and software, went from its founding in 2001 to exceeding $1 billion in revenue in 2005. iPhone app sales reached a billion dollars in a matter of years.

Accelerated Darwinism means companies can explode or implode almost overnight.

Certainly other factors and causes beyond Accelerated Darwinism are in play as well. Hype—or over-hype—is often a causal factor in company or even industry growth. Technology makes it much easier to quickly build a big company but also makes sustaining that company much more difficult as well.

The first to market does not necessarily win in the short or long term—the first to truly understand the needs and expectations of the customer and to meet those needs and expectations wins.

The iPhone was not the first smart phone but quickly became the most popular (at least for a time.) Google wasn't the first search engine. Amazon wasn't the first online retailer. MS-DOS wasn't the first PC operating system and Windows wasn't the first graphical user interface operating system. Instead, research shows customers are incredibly satisfied with Apple, Google, Amazon, and Microsoft allowing those companies to stay on top more easily.

When customer needs shift and evolve the competition accelerates. The winner is the business that meets the needs, exceeds the expectations, and best satisfies the customer.

Consider another industry, one familiar to almost everyone: social media. MySpace was a major player but is now largely irrelevant; Friendster was there before MySpace. If you want to join a social network today to connect with your friends, peers, and colleagues, Facebook is the place to be—at least as this book is written—not Friendster or MySpace. Facebook has enjoyed a near-monopoly on a segment of social media for several years, but its popularity seems to be peaking. Although for some this may be hard to imagine, the future of Facebook is far from guaranteed.

Facebook is so important that in 2010 it was added to the list of companies measured by the American Customer Satisfaction Index (ACSI). Findings were odd, especially considering

Facebook's popularity. In July of 2011 the ACSI score for Facebook was 66, around ten points below the national average and trailing organizations like Burger King, Bank of America, and even the Internal Revenue Service.

Why? Consumers were upset about privacy issues, a frequently changing user interface, and the "commercialization" of Facebook. Absent customer satisfaction improvements, when consumers have viable options they will leave Facebook for those options.

With the entry of Google+ in mid-2011 a real social media shakeup could be in the works. In fact, Google+ is a perfect example of Accelerated Darwinism. Google+ acquired twenty million users in less than a month even while technically still in beta. Facebook and Twitter required years to achieve the same milestone.

MySpace rose in popularity but over the long term failed to meet customer needs. Super Consumers made MySpace. They just as easily broke MySpace, a business bought for $580M in 2005 and eventually sold in 2011 for a paltry $35M. Super Consumers can break Facebook, too.

Super Consumers have the power to take companies from zero to billions—and back.

That, in a nutshell, is Accelerated Darwinism.

Bottom line? Over time the balance of power will continue to shift in favor of the consumer. Fail to listen to your customers and that shifting balance of power will catch you by surprise—and dramatically impact your long-term chances for survival of the corporate fittest.

There is, however, a way to restore the balance of power and actually take advantage of the emergence of the Super Consumer.

To restore the balance of power, companies must know as much as possible about what customers know, what customers want, and what drives customer behavior. Companies must know as much about consumers as they know about the companies, products, and services they choose to spend their time and money on.

In short, we do not need to take power away from the consumer. Even if we wanted to, taking power away from the consumer is neither possible nor the point. Consumer power is here—and is here to stay.

To survive and thrive in the age of Accelerated Darwinism, businesses must recognize the power of the consumer and harness that power to meet or exceed ever-changing expectations while at the same time growing and sustaining a profitable business. The companies that can best enable consumers to flex their increasing power are the companies that will prosper. Companies that fail to do so (as determined by their customers, not by internal opinions and self-proclaimed experts) simply cannot succeed.

Businesses that drive customer satisfaction drive their own financial success. But how can companies drive online customer satisfaction? Which metrics will help identify and prioritize what kinds of improvements need to be made in order to increase satisfaction, and therefore revenue, profitability, and growth? These are the questions businesses must answer to succeed in the Customer 2.0 marketplace.

# chapter 3

# DATA IN A VACUUM:

## THE CHALLENGE OF BEHAVIORAL DATA

**W**hen you have nothing, having something—having *any-thing*—can start to look really good. Small advances can seem like large advances. Minor changes can seem like major changes. It is easy to say, "Look how far we've come!" when you start with almost nothing.

In the early days of the Internet, especially where data collection and web analytics were concerned, that is precisely the phenomenon that took place. Even with the sophisticated technological advances now at our disposal, in many ways that legacy continues. You cannot blame the early pioneers; they used the data that was available (along with a healthy dose of trial and error) to drive decisions.

But that approach does not provide the insights a business needs to manage forward.

Let's look at a few examples that point out the challenges of behavioral data.

# Getting "Sticky"

In the pre-Accelerated Darwinism, pre-Web 2.0, pre-Super Consumer business world, a primary business goal was to find ways to make the customer "stick" to the environment.

The goal of a typical department store or retail outlet was to keep you in the store for as long as possible. The longer you stayed the greater the likelihood you would make a purchase, whether due to sales pressure or simply because you had already "invested" a lot of time in the process of shopping at that store. In media terms, the goal of a TV network was to keep you on that channel so their ratings would be higher. The same was true with radio stations, hence the importance of "day parts" and quarter-hours.

Stickiness worked. Due to the cost of switching—even if switching only meant picking up a different magazine or driving to another bank branch or walking across the street to a different shoe store—the likelihood of achieving business success by creating a sticky environment was extremely high.

Today the word "sticky" has come to mean many things, especially in online marketing terms, but for our purposes we will use the term to refer to how a website holds visitor attention and why visitors spend longer periods of time on a site.

The underlying assumption was that if users were "stuck" on a website, they could not be anywhere else. That seemed like a good idea at the time because the theory worked in other channels. Conventional wisdom assumed the longer a visitor remained on a website the better. Businesses applied pre-Accelerated Darwinism concepts to the emerging Internet environment.

Unfortunately the concept of "stickiness" does not apply in today's web world and, even if it once did, is inherently difficult to force in the online environment. In fact, trying to force stickiness on users often has the reverse effect, driving them away from a site. With switching costs low and competition high, there are many other sites for them to visit.

And visit those sites they will. Make them stick to your site against their will, by forcing more navigation to find desired results or by unnecessarily spreading content or search results across multiple pages, and visitors quickly go elsewhere.

Measurements designed to measure and evaluate stickiness in Internet terms are still commonly referenced and widely used, despite the fact the stickiness paradigm is at best suspect and at worst tremendously harmful in an Accelerated Darwinism business world. The main problem is that sticky measurements are strictly behavioral and therefore often misleading.

So why do we try to replicate such a quintessentially offline concept in an online environment?

Take a simple and widely used behavioral web metric many companies use to evaluate the success, failure, and stickiness of a website: page views. Each time a visitor views a page on your website a page view is generated. Say three months ago visitors to your site viewed an average of five pages before exiting. Was that good? Was that poor?

In the absence of other data it is hard to tell, so you wisely decide to measure trends over time in order to gauge site performance and evaluate the results of changes made to your site. Over the course of several months you spend thousands of dollars on site modifications. After the changes are complete, you run analytics on the previous month's visitors and find your page view average has decreased to from five pages to three pages per visitor.

What happened? You spent thousands of dollars, put major time and effort into your site...and found out you are worse off than when you started. After all, page views decreased, right? Your site was less sticky, not more.

Possibly so.

But possibly your changes resulted in greater visitor satisfaction. Stickiness could be irrelevant depending on the needs and expectations of your visitors.

I realize linking fewer average page views with higher satisfaction seems counterintuitive. For some businesses that assumption may be incorrect, which is why using deeper metrics is necessary. Still, satisfaction is a result of how an experience compares to expectations. If a visitor is more satisfied because she found exactly what she wanted within three page views, the result is increased loyalty and more recommendations to your site and your business.

In the meantime, your web analysts view a decline in page views as a major failure of the website upgrades.

Here's an example. I received my undergraduate degree from the University of Michigan. I live in Ann Arbor and my family has season tickets to Michigan football games. I follow Michigan football closely. Imagine one Sunday morning I want to check a few stats to settle a friendly wager with one of my sons. I go to the Michigan football home page, MGoBlue.com, click a couple of links, and within seconds find exactly what I want to know: Tshimanga Biakabutuka rushed for 313 yards against Ohio State on November 25, 1995, the second highest yards ever gained by a Michigan running back in one game. The Michigan Wolverines won that game 31–23. Those were the days! (We Michigan fans hope to return to those days soon.)

But I only viewed three pages.

Following the stickiness paradigm could lead you to believe the Michigan football website does a terrible job of creating a sticky environment. I viewed three pages. I didn't stay. I didn't browse. I didn't consume page after page after page. I was on the website for seconds, not minutes.

But think about what *really* happened. What was my intent? My intent was to find a specific football statistic. Did I find the stat I was looking for? Yes, quickly and easily. While I only viewed three pages I was highly satisfied by my experience, especially because it only took a couple of clicks to find what I wanted. My intent was to find a few stats; my expectation was finding those stats would be easy and straightforward.

That is exactly what happened.

Measuring my page views, and *only* my page views, in no way indicates my level of satisfaction, my likelihood of returning to the site, my likelihood of purchasing a Michigan football jersey...in fact my likelihood of taking *any* future action.

My page view statistics indicate only one thing: I viewed three pages. Observation of my actions cannot provide insight into my level of satisfaction. Satisfaction cannot be measured by observation.

I was satisfied. I will be loyal. I will be back, and I will recommend the site to others (by the way, you really should check out MGoBlue.com!)

On the other hand, what if finding the stats I wanted meant sifting through fifteen or twenty pages and spending five or ten frustrating minutes on the site? Measured in a vacuum, without consideration of intent or expectation or future behaviors, that type of visit to the could easily be considered a smashing success based on the high number of page views and the lengthy amount of time I spent on the site.

Great—but since I was not satisfied by my visit I may never return. I have too many options at my disposal. Technology allows me to be on multiple sites at the same time, and any number of sports and information websites contain the same basic information and statistics. Plus, my switching costs are nonexistent. Exiting the site, never to return, is for me a zero-cost action.

The same holds true for virtually all kinds of websites and businesses. If retail sites follow a stickiness paradigm and use traditional web analytics—like time on site and pages viewed—to measure site success, their chances of performing an accurate analysis are hardly better than flipping a coin. The intent of my visit is critical and cannot be determined by simply observing where I visited and what I did.

Using traditional metrics like page views makes it very hard to know if your web efforts are successful. While page view metrics may manage to accurately count page views, the data gathered is neither insightful nor meaningful in a world of Accelerated Darwinism.

The issue becomes more complicated when users access your site from different devices. Unless they log on to your website you have no way to tell if they are the same user, further complicating measurement and minimizing the value of behavioral data alone. I may visit your site from my laptop, my iPhone, my iPad, from the four other computers in the house, on my Google TV, and in the future from my car, my refrigerator . . . and who knows where else. Today's consumer is not only multichannel but also multi-device.

In simple terms, satisfied visitors and satisfied customers spend more time on a site and with a brand over a long period of time—not necessarily for a long time on one visit. Think of this premise as the lifetime value of a site visitor. The true value of a visitor cannot be measured in one session, in one day, or in one week.

# Bounce Rate

Bounce rate is another useful but generally misapplied web metric.

Bounce rate calculates the percentage of visitors who view one page and then "bounce" off that page to a different site instead of viewing additional pages on the original site. Exit rate, sometimes called page exit ratio, is a similar metric that measures the percentage of visitors who leave a site from individual pages. (By definition all visitors eventually exit but not all visitors bounce.)

Bounce rate is calculated by dividing the total number of visits into the total number of visitors who view one page. If 1,000 people visit and 200 leave after viewing one page, the bounce rate is 20%.

Exit rate is calculated by dividing the total number of visitors to a page into the total number of visitors who exit the site after viewing that page. If 1,000 people view a page and 400 leave after viewing that page, the exit rate for that specific page is 40%.

The traditional use of these two metrics assumes the lower the bounce rate and exit rate, the better. Why? While there are a variety of theories, viewed in customer satisfaction terms, the basic assumption is that unsatisfied visitors bounce or exit.

That assumption is not always correct. The traditional view of these metrics does not take into account the impact of visitor intent, especially in a multichannel world. Many companies assume the pages on their sites with the highest exit rates need to be "fixed." But say a customer visits a product page, finds the information she wants (say a product price), and exits so she can drive to the store and pick the item up in person. Should the page be "fixed"? Was she dissatisfied by her visit to the website? Hardly—she found exactly what she was looking for.

She left after viewing one page *because* she was satisfied—based on her original intent.

In many cases the page with the highest exit rate is the page that best meets visitor needs and expectations. To truly understand behavioral metrics like bounce rate or exit rate, other factors—like initial intent and subsequent actions—must be taken into account. Otherwise you may fix what is not broken and ignore what may be, in fact, a real problem...and a real opportunity for improvement.

Data does not equal actionable intelligence, especially when you jump to conclusions or simply follow conventional wisdom based on that data—no matter how accurate the metric itself may be.

### Conventional Wisdom Does Not Equal Wise Decisions

A great example of the perils of following conventional wisdom can be found in Michael Lewis's book Moneyball. Moneyball describes how Billy Beane and the Oakland A's revolutionized the way traditional baseball statistics and performance metrics can be used to evaluate player performance and build a better team. While Moneyball is at heart a baseball book, it is also an outstanding business book that shows how limited resources can be leveraged by using intelligent analysis and out-of-the-box thinking.

For years general managers and coaches have used traditional statistics like runs batted in and batting average to evaluate player performance. A player's batting average is determined by dividing the total number of at-bats (excluding walks and sacrifices) into the number of hits. For example, a player averaging .300 or better (three hits out of ten at bats) is performing well.

Beane realized that on base percentage, the percentage of time a player reaches base through either a walk or hit, is actually a much greater factor for determining team success. In simple terms, the more base runners the greater the likelihood a team will score runs, and runs win games.

Batting averages provide a window into individual performance. On-base percentage provides a much sharper and more predictive look at key success drivers.

Web analytics are useful. Traditional metrics are useful. But no business can afford to base an assessment or judgment on one statistic. Beane took traditional metrics and applied them differently to make decisions based on metrics that could better predict the future.

Beane took information and turned it into intelligence. He gained a competitive advantage by utilizing metrics and analytics in the right way.

The key is to use traditional metrics wisely, which is often not as easy as it sounds.

# Shopping Cart Abandonment

Shopping cart abandonment is another classic example of a frequently misused metric.

Shopping cart abandonment rate is calculated by dividing the number of visitors who start but then abandon a shopping cart (in other words, who do not complete the transaction) by the total number of visitors who initially create a shopping cart.

Abandoned shopping carts are the bane of an e-commerce site's existence. (Picture business owners thinking about high shopping cart abandon rates; if you imagine them with their heads in hands crying, *"Why?"* you're not too far off the mark. After all, *"They were this close...and then they left..."*)

A business that knows you abandoned your shopping cart can certainly infer you were not satisfied with some portion of the shopping or checkout process. Maybe you could not easily delete an item you no longer wanted. Maybe you could not determine the shipping cost for your order. Maybe you felt there were too many steps to the process and got frustrated.

Or maybe you never intended to buy at all and were only having fun doing a little virtual window-shopping.

Instead of attempting to *infer* what happened and why, the business should instead *ask* you about your experience. A business that knows why you abandoned and what you plan to do as a result of abandoning can then start to understand your needs and expectations as a customer. A business that knows the causal factors behind your actions can determine what to do as a result—and can predict the results of changes made to better satisfy you as a customer.

That is why behavioral data can be misleading, especially in extreme circumstances.

While it may come as a surprise to some readers, many times when companies are struggling or even near bankruptcy their customer satisfaction rates actually go up instead of down. Does that make intuitive sense, especially since financial performance and stock prices tend to rise in conjunction with rising satisfaction rates?

Of course not—it is easy to assume struggling companies are the last companies with satisfied customers.

But that assumption is also wrong, since often the only customers left are loyal customers who remain loyal because, for whatever reason, they are still satisfied. Kmart is a prime example of a company that entered bankruptcy in 2002 even after a period of rising customer satisfaction. (I like to think of this phenomenon as the "mother's love" syndrome. No matter what other people think your mother still loves you.)

The same phenomenon occurred at AOL. Customer satisfaction increased in 2005 and 2006 while the total number of customers decreased. Customers left in droves to take advantage of free services, and AOL's for-pay model was no longer relevant to any but the most die-hard AOL user.

Die-hards were satisfied; die-hards were the only users left; satisfaction rates increased.

# Backwards-Looking Metrics

At some point every day I say, "You cannot manage what you do not measure." The success of our company—and the success of our clients—is based on that premise. We live by that statement and everything it stands for.

The problem is that most metrics and measurement tools look backwards. The accounting discipline itself is, out of necessity, based on backwards reporting. Even sophisticated financial analysts use backwards-looking metrics.

For example, Wall Street bases company valuations and evaluates financial performance by using accounting measures that in large part look back rather than forward. (One exception is an earnings estimate, which is a prediction often used more in an attempt to manage market expectations than as a tool for truly managing company strategy and predicting future company performance.)

Looking back is fine, but what most financial analysts lack is the data needed to translate historical results in order to predict the future.

Think about it. What really predicts the future? How many customers you had...or how many customers you will have?

How many products you sold last year, or how many products you will sell in the coming year? Do you wish you could confidently predict how many customers you will have and how much you will sell next year? Of course you do; then you could confidently make important strategic and tactical decisions on capital investments, staffing, inventory planning, and more.

In web terms, most companies use backwards-looking measurements like churn rate, revenue per customer, and new customer acquisition rates. These and a host of other metrics are important and should be tracked and analyzed, but each also looks backwards instead of forward.

It is great if you know what your churn rate has been or what your revenue per customer has been—but that does not mean you understand what your data indicates going forward.

# Performance vs. Success

Key *performance* indicators based on past results provide valuable information and definitely should not be ignored. Examples of key performance indicators include site performance, page views, unique visitors, conversion rate, and abandonment rate.

Key *success* indicators measure *success* rather than just *performance*.

Some metrics fit into both categories, and some clearly do not. Does a fast-loading page indicate success? What about the number of unique visitors? While these are important metrics, an increase or decrease in results does not indicate success or failure. Reducing page load times from an average of 1.2 seconds to 1 second is definitely a positive change—but that change alone will not cause a site visitor to consider her experience a success. On the other hand, if your page load times increase from 1.2 seconds to 8 seconds your visitor may definitely consider her experience a failure—and so will you.

Often metrics are more indicative of performance than success. Which are you most concerned with? If you are concerned with success, track success indicators instead of performance indicators alone.

A critical key success indicator is customer satisfaction, the ultimate measurement of success. Satisfied customers (and visitors, prospects, and users) become long-term, loyal, and profitable customers—and will recommend you to others. Those outcomes create success both for your customers and for your business.

A dissatisfied customer is not likely to be a long-term or loyal customer. Consumers go where they are satisfied. Dissatisfied customers will go elsewhere as soon as they find a viable or even semi-viable alternative, turning your original cost of acquisition into a sunk cost rather than an investment. Dissatisfied customers may also generate negative word of mouth and magnify the cost of their dissatisfaction. When that happens, a dissatisfied customer becomes both a cost and a liability.

And speaking of liabilities, a company's balance sheet contains a breakdown of its assets, liabilities, and owner or stockholder equity. Since an asset is anything a business owns that has monetary value, satisfied customers are a missing asset class on every balance sheet.

Why? What truly drives future results? Your company's most important asset is not your location, your technology, your website, or even your employees (although employees come a very close second.)

Your most important business asset is your customers. Without customers every other asset is irrelevant. Let's look at a hypothetical business to illustrate the point.

Say a mainstream multichannel retailer, "Company X," has in recent years dramatically increased their online marketing efforts with mixed results. As a marketing consultant you are asked to help Company X determine the best websites to place their banner ads.

If you decide to take a simplistic, pre-Accelerated Darwinism approach, you will look at what already happened on websites where you are considering advertising in order to choose the best options.

You might look at metrics like:

> Average page views, to determine how many pages the average visitor views

> Average time on site, to determine how long, in minutes and seconds, the average visitor stays on that site

> Number of unique visitors, to determine how many individual visitors come to the site (after factoring out return visitors)

Those metrics do provide a sense of the size of a site's audience as well as some of the behaviors of that audience, like how the number of pages they visit and how long they stay. Since Website A has more page views, more average time spent on site, and more visitors than Website B, you recommend buying banner advertising on Website A. Why? Conventional wisdom assumes the bigger the audience the longer they stay on site, and the more pages they view the better the website for advertisers.

But conventional assumptions are not always right and do not always reflect the deeper truth. An equally important factor—or perhaps even more important factor—is whether or not Website A and Website B create a satisfied audience. The association of Company X with a smaller but satisfied audience helps them far more than advertising on a "bad" site with lots of visitors who have a poor experience and never return. In effect the company could suffer from "guilt" (a word used very loosely) by association with a poor site. Size of site and number of visitors are important criteria—but the quality of the site is as important, if not more important.

A similar lack of long-term focus happens frequently. As mentioned earlier, some advertisers only care about eyeballs. Visitors, page views, and time on site means everything. Hundreds of thousands of site visitors may indeed create broader brand exposure, but at what cost and what negative association if the site creates a poor visitor experience?

Keep in mind considerations like these do not occur in a vacuum. Exposure to thousands of visitors can create an incredible audience for your message. Visitors who stay on a site for a long period of time may encounter your banner ad more often and may be more likely to click through to your site.

Value is created for advertisers through exposure and click-throughs. Dwelling on a particular site is not a bad thing, but staying on a "bad" site can be a terrible outcome when your brand suffers by association.

## Web Advertising

Exposure and click-throughs drive revenue for content publishers. In web advertising multiple revenue models are used; the most common are cost per thousand, cost per click, and cost per action.

Under cost per thousand models, an advertiser is charged based on the number of times a banner ad is "delivered" to a visitor (even if the visitor never noticed the ad.) Cost per click charges the advertiser when a visitor clicks on an ad; this approach is most commonly used in sponsored listings like Google AdWords. Cost per action or per acquisition models charge the advertiser when a visitor takes a specific action, like making a purchase, completing a form, or registering on an adver-tiser's site. Because cost per action is based on measur-able outcomes the cost per action rate is naturally higher.

Now think about your brand, and in a larger sense your website or your business. Is it better to advertise to Visitor A, a person who sees your ad ten times during one web session but is dissatisfied and never returns? Or is it better to advertise to Visitor B, a person who is satisfied and views one page but continues to view one page a week for an entire year?

Again, consider the situation using a traditional metric like average page views. Using conventional logic, Visitor A is more "valuable" because he or she saw your ad ten times in a month. Visitor B is theoretically less valuable in the short run. You value Visitor A because you delivered ten page views that month instead of only four.

In the long run, however, you should value Visitor B more highly because Visitor B results in fifty-two total page views. Plus, Visitor B saw those ads on a site where they had a better experience and were more satisfied.

Satisfaction breeds loyalty. Loyalty creates long-term customers and consumers. Using traditional metrics alone can cause you to take a short-term approach and therefore advertise on the wrong types of sites for your business. The better the site, the better your advertising is perceived.

What constitutes a "better" site? The number of page views? Absolutely not, since any business can *buy* page views. Traditional metrics provide important data, like visitor counts and visitor demographics, but without an accurate way to measure visitor satisfaction you only receive a portion of the information you really need to make smart decisions.

# Measure All Customer Touch Points

Another challenge of behavioral metrics is their inability to measure or shed light on the cross-channel customer experience. Businesses can no longer afford to only think in terms of separate silos having separate impacts on consumers. We must measure the impact of each and every touch point with consumers: physical locations, call centers, web, mobile, and social network interactions all must be measured not only as individual channels but as they combine to enhance or detract from overall brand affinity. Behavioral data often does not know where a visitor comes from, where a visitor goes, or if an individual visitor is the same person visiting from multiple devices.

Imagine the intelligence and competitive advantage you can gain if you truly understand how each consumer touch point meets customer needs and expectations. If you simply understand customer satisfaction at an aggregate level you gain certainly gain insight, but that insight is difficult to make actionable. If you understand customer satisfaction during each interaction and experience with consumers, you can turn insight into actionable intelligence and create a true competitive advantage.

# chapter 4

# CUSTOMER INTENT AND TRUE CONVERSION RATE

A discussion of customer intent could easily have fallen in the previous chapter, but such a major topic deserves special focus, especially as it applies to conversion rate.

Conversion rate is one of the most commonly misused behavioral metrics. Conversion rate measures the number of visitors to a particular web site, within a specific period, divided into the number of people who take the desired action (make a purchase, register for a free trial, or any other intended action.)

---

Conversion rate =
# of visitors who convert/total number of visitors

---

Many web-based businesses feel conversion rate is the most if not only important metric. Why? In financial terms, conversion rate can spell the difference between business success and failure.

What constitutes a "good" conversion rate depends on the industry and the nature of the action desired. According to Forrester Research, the average conversion rate for a typical e-commerce site is approximately 3.5%. While I trust Forrester's data completely, in and of itself a 3.5% average conversion rate is a misleading benchmark to apply.

Say in your industry conversion rates typically fall between 3 and 5%. In that case a 2% conversion rate is considered poor and a 10% conversion rate is outstanding. You run a marketing campaign, spend $20,000 on that campaign, and drive 10,000 new visitors to your site. Your average customer spends $200.

Why does conversion rate matter so much?

| If your conversion rate is | You acquired | At an acquisition cost/ customer of | Generating revenue of |
|---|---|---|---|
| 2% | 200 customers | $100 | $40,000 |
| 3% | 300 customers | $66.67 | $60,000 |
| 5% | 500 customers | $40 | $100,000 |
| 10% | 1,000 customers | $20 | $200,000 |

As conversion rates go up revenues rise while marketing costs (as a percentage of total sales) fall. That is why conversion rates tend to matter so much, and why conversion rate is a basic web analytics tool. Conversion rate matters because it directly impacts revenue and the cost of customer acquisition.

At the same time, focusing solely on an aggregate conversion rate can be misleading. Say you implement a marketing campaign that places TV and print ads in locations where you do not have physical locations. After implementing your campaign you realize your website conversion rate has decreased.

Taken at face value the new marketing campaign appears to be the direct cause of a lower conversion rate. But maybe not: what was the *real* cause of the decreased conversion rate? And what was the goal of your campaign?

Possibly your goal was to attract a total new audience segment to your site, an audience segment largely unfamiliar with your brand. If your conversion rate before the campaign was 4% and the visitors who arrived as a result of the campaign converted at a 2% rate, the result at an aggregate level is a lower conversion rate.

But what really happened is that new visitors to your site as a result of the campaign naturally converted at a lower rate, bringing the aggregate down—even though a greater number of total visitors did convert.

That kind of result is not necessarily poor or even surprising. We often find that new visitors, especially those unfamiliar with a brand, will convert at a lower rate than existing customers. The net business impact is positive—more people buy products—but using that ever-important behavioral metric, conversion rate, generates misleading information.

Since conversion rate is the ratio of the total number of people who performed a desired action divided by the total number of visitors, *why* people visited your website is another critical piece of information often missing.

Say you manufacture and sell exterior doors and you add comprehensive service and repair information to your website. Now visitors can quickly find information to make basic home repairs on your products. Over time, more and more visitors seek that information, and your total number of site visitors increases. If the total number of conversions remains flat your conversion rate will naturally decrease. It would be easy to assume that since the conversion rate dropped after changes were made to the website, making those changes was a mistake.

Easy to assume—and wrong.

While the conversion rate of total site visitors declined, the decline was the result of the additional visitors who came for support information. The conversion rate of visitors arriving to purchase remained the same—and in addition you now provide a better experience for customers seeking support. While the rate of visitors who made a purchase decreased, overall customer satisfaction is likely higher because people who expected to receive maintenance information were in fact able to find the information they sought. Not only will those visitors be more satisfied, the result should be lower support costs elsewhere in your organization (like in your call centers, for example).

In this case you don't actually mind a lower overall conversion rate; in fact, you welcome that result. But at first glance not everyone in your organization will be as happy to see your conversion rate decline.

Here is a final example. Consider what typically happens when a retailer introduces a new product or product line. Say an online electronics retailer has never sold cell phones but adds the product line to its stores. In order to drive traffic the retailer naturally uses a variety of advertising tools.

Potential new customers who arrive as a result of advertising are unlikely to convert at as high a rate as "normal" site visitors; "normal" site visitors tend to be repeat customers already familiar with the retailer's products and services.

As a result, the aggregate conversion rate will naturally decrease.

Does a decreased aggregate conversion rate indicate the decision to expand into the cell phone market was poor? No—the result simply means those sales occur at a lower rate of conversion.

New visitors do not convert at the same rate as long-term visitors. If you only evaluate aggregate conversion rate you may assume—incorrectly—your efforts were unsuccessful.

# True Conversion Rate

That is why the metric you truly care about is your True Conversion rate. As a business you care about the number of visitors who came to your site intending to make a purchase *who did in fact make that purchase*. The same is true with the visitors who came to your site seeking support information. You care about the number of visitors who came to your site looking for information who were, in fact, able to find the information they sought.

True Conversion starts with determining your specific goals and only then moves to measuring the customer's intent. For example, in most cases your goal is for visitors to perform a specific action. If you are a retailer, your goal is for visitors to buy a product. If you focus on lead generation, your goal is for visitors to become a lead. If you publish a newsletter, your goal is for visitors to sign up for that newsletter. If you run a bank, your goal may be for visitors to open a new account, sign up for online banking, or pay a bill online.

Regardless of your industry, you must first clearly define your goals. What do you most want visitors to do on your site? If you do not define your goals you cannot measure success or failure.

Then, when you attract a new visitor you must understand the visitor's intentions. That is the only way to calculate a True Conversion rate as well as they only way to understand customer satisfaction.

Here is an example. To keep things simple we will assume you are a multichannel retailer and your website is designed to provide two basic services. You seek to sell products and to provide support for customers who purchase products.

Those are your goals, but visitors naturally come to your site for different reasons. Some come to purchase, others come to do research for a potential future purchase, and some come for support. Support may include getting instructions or maintenance information on products that have been purchased, checking on the status of an order, or simply searching for a store location.

In fact, research we conducted at ForeSee to evaluate the forty largest online retailers during the 2010 holiday season showed that 47% of visitors came to those sites with the intent of researching, 38% came with the intent to purchase, and 15% came with other intentions like product support or order status checks.

While you built your site for two main purposes, visitors actually come for three main reasons.

So let's take a closer look at those three reasons. The first segment, the visitors who arrive intending to make a purchase, fall directly in your sweet spot. Your objective and consumer objectives match.

Is a 3 to 5% conversion rate acceptable under these circumstances? Absolutely not: When a visitor comes to your site intending to purchase you should expect conversion rates to be higher than single digits. We see True Conversion rates (based on visitors who arrive with intent to purchase) as high as 40% depending on the company and the industry. When visitors come to your online store with purchases in their eyes and credit cards in their hands, non-conversions are failures.

The second segment, visitors who arrive to research a product for a potential later purchase, is also a group we hope to convert. However, converting these visitors is a much more difficult task, so our expectations should be reasonable. We will likely see low single digit, near-zero conversion rates for this group. Our objective then is to meet the customer needs and exceed customer expectations—to satisfy the customer.

The consumer determines success; we do not. Did visitors find the information they wanted to find? A satisfying experience could potentially lead to an immediate purchase, but a future purchase is more likely, whether from our website or from a retail store. Success for this segment cannot be measured by purchase alone or by other behavioral measurements.

The third segment, the visitors who arrive for support, has no intention of making a purchase. Any conversion from this group is a bonus. Our goal is to satisfy these visitors in order to increase their likelihood of becoming loyal customers and making a purchase in the future. Hopefully these visitors will also recommend us to others. Plus, they could possibly decrease our overall support costs, since the support they receive is online instead of through more costly channels like a call center.

Now look at numbers. If a thousand people visit our site and forty made a purchase, our aggregate conversion rate is 4%.

Then drill down into segments. What is our True Conversion rate? If three hundred of our visitors arrived with the intent to purchase and we converted thirty-six of those visitors, our True Conversion rate is 12%.

If four hundred arrived to do research and we converted six of those visitors, our conversion rate is 1.5% for this segment.

If none of the three hundred that came for support converted, our conversion rate is 0%.

Here are the results:

| Intent of Visit | Visitors | Conversions | Conversion Rate |
| --- | --- | --- | --- |
| Purchase | 300 | 36 | 12% |
| Research | 400 | 6 | 1.5% |
| Support | 300 | 0 | 0% |
| Total | 1,000 | 42 | 4.2% |

Our True Conversion rate was 12%. True Conversion is a far more useful metric than an aggregate conversion rate of 3.5%.

What did we learn? First, conversion rate alone is not a measure of success. Is a 1.5% conversion rate a good or bad result for our "researching" segment? There is no way to tell by evaluating conversion rate alone. What we must know is whether visitors were satisfied and whether they are likely to purchase from us in the future, either online or offline. The long-term value created from positive consumer experiences can be far more important to our business than the short-term value.

Success in our support segment cannot be measured by visitor behavior or conversion. Success should be measured by the satisfaction level of those visitors and by their future likely behaviors, such as whether they will recommend us to others, continue to use the online channel for support, or purchase more from us in the future. In other words, we must use different success metrics than conversion rate to evaluate visitors who arrived with no intent of making a purchase.

The True Conversion metric provides a better and more accurate measurement of success. Use voice of customer research to find out why the customer came in the first place and whether they were satisfied; combine this information with behavioral data to find out whether they made a purchase. Then you can transform conversion rate, a fundamentally misleading measurement, into a meaningful metric.

## How to Measure Customer Intent and the Multichannel Consumer

We gauge customer intent by conducting initial surveys followed up by subsequent surveys that comprehensively evaluate the overall process and customer experience—including a methodology to determine which actions the respondent took as the result of their visit. In a multichannel world we must measure all customer touch points and fully understand the relationship between those touch points.

The process of determining customer satisfaction starts with intentions and ends with outcomes. Our goal is to understand intentions and expectations, understand whether and to what extent those intentions and expectations were met, and determine what the customer actually did as a result of their visit or experience.

There are five possible outcomes a multichannel retailer:

1. The customer made no purchase

2. The customer made the purchase from the retailer online

3. The customer made the purchase from the retailer offline

4. The customer made the purchase from a competitor online

5. The customer made the purchase from a competitor offline

This approach applies to a broader range of behaviors and outcomes than within retail activity alone. "Purchase" can take on different meanings. If your goal, for example, is to sign up new members, that action can be considered a "purchase" even if no money changes hands. Or say you run a government agency and your goal is for citizens to fill out Social Security benefit applications online as opposed to in person at a local office; a successfully completed application can be considered a "purchase."

Potential outcomes can vary, but those different outcomes are easy to define based on your particular business model. As an example, where Social Security benefit applications are concerned the potential outcomes are "Applied online," "Applied offline," and, "Did not apply."

A manufacturer with an online channel that also sells to retailers for online and offline distribution has six potential outcomes:

1. Purchased online directly from manufacturer

2. Purchased the manufacturer's product online from a retailer

3. Purchased the manufacturer's product offline from a retailer

4. Purchased a competitor's product online

5. Purchased a competitor's product offline

6. Did not purchase

By asking what actually occurred after and as a result of a visit—no purchase, purchase online, purchase from a competitor, etc.—we can determine what really happened and how truly satisfied customers were with their experience.

Traditional metrics are flawed because they only take into account behaviors. The only way to truly understand customer satisfaction is to employ a methodology that captures the voice of customer.

Listening to customers helps identify intent and as a result is a key component used to evaluate whether you satisfy your customers, whether your customers will be loyal, whether your customers will recommend you to others, and whether your customers will return. We never *infer* satisfaction, loyalty, or intentions from correlated data—we go right to the source and ask. Understanding intent and outcomes using a scientific methodology allows us to determine causal factors that predict the future instead of relying on correlations that may not predict anything at all.

To illustrate the point let's look at conversion rates again, only this time in a different way. Say overall conversion rates at your company have remained static for years. Relatively flat results make sense if for no other reason than the weight of statistical data; when you look at results in aggregate, the needle is incredibly hard to move. Turning an oil tanker on a dime is impossible.

So what can you do? Instead of trying to move the aggregate, segment your audience and your customers like we did in the earlier example. Determine which people come to your store or site to make a purchase...and make sure you do the right things to enable them to make that purchase. Determine which people look for product or service information and do the right things to provide that information...quickly and conveniently.

The goal is to increase the conversion rate, for the audience that can be converted, based on their intent. Make changes and evaluate the success of those changes.

Then you may need to take the process a step farther. Consider segmenting intent by the source of acquisition. Was the visit due to awareness of your brand, to a recommendation from a friend, or to offline or digital advertising or search? Understanding how you attracted a visitor to your site or how you acquired that visitor can be an illuminating segmentation to layer onto initial intent segmentation.

With the right data you can turn data into intelligence and determine that while your overall conversion rate may have decreased...your True Conversion rate actually increased.

Traditional metrics and traditional measurements are useful and important, but often also leave out a key indicator of overall performance. My guess is you use a number of traditional metrics. And you should.

# Improving Conversion and True Conversion Rates

What does our research show leads to solid online conversion rates?

The answer varies enormously from business to business depending on your site, your product mix, your positioning, your customers, your competition, and a number of other attributes. But there are a few common themes that emerge from the millions of consumers we have studied regarding key drivers.

## Content and/or Merchandise

Regardless of the type of site, ultimately the information contained on your site makes a big impact on conversion rates. This includes information like content for news and information sites; merchandise information for retailers; product information for product sites; and help and information (like frequently asked questions or FAQs) for support sites.

## Ease of Use

Sites that are easy to use and easy to navigate typically result in higher conversion rates. Confusing, difficult to navigate sites generally result in lower conversion rates. Due to low switching costs and increased competition, when visitors cannot figure out how to navigate a site to quickly find what they need they go elsewhere.

## Price

Price can have an impact on conversion rates. In the early days of the web, a time that promised increased competition between businesses and greater choices for consumers, many speculated the Internet would turn most items into a commodity and price would be the dominant driver of consumer decisions. That speculation proved to be inaccurate. We have seen the relationship of price to conversion vary greatly between businesses and evolve over time as the economic environment evolves.

## Site Performance

Slow, buggy, error-prone sites lead to lower conversion rates even if price and quality are competitive. However, we typically see a cliff effect when we analyze site performance. There is an acceptable level of performance from a user's perspective (which varies from user to user), so as long as the site performs at or better than that an expected performance level there is very little impact on conversion rates. When performance does not measure up to an "acceptable" level, that poor performance often has an extremely negative impact on conversion rates.

## Functionality

Overall convenience of a site is important, including factors like whether the site provides functionalities the user wants or needs. One good example is the Amazon "1-Click" ordering function: find a product, click the "1-Click" button, and credit card and delivery address information previously stored is used to generate the order.

Make the process convenient and conversion rates tend to increase. The ability to customize content, configure products, read reviews by other customers, change product colors, and check product availability are some of the functions users expect from leading websites—and from your site.

## Effective Marketing

Visitors who come to your site seeking what you provide tend to convert at a higher rate; if your advertising materials are unclear or in any way misleading (even if unintentionally) many visitors leave because the site did not meet the expectations set by your marketing efforts. Marketing, in conjunction with prior perception, in large part sets consumer expectations. If the marketing is misleading the experience will not meet expectations. Customers will be dissatisfied and will not convert. Effective advertising yields targeted traffic; the less targeted your traffic the less likely visitors will be to convert.

## Customer Satisfaction

Each of the previous drivers impact whether consumers are satisfied. If consumers are satisfied they are more likely to convert. Factors like content/merchandise, ease of use, price, functionality, performance, and effective marketing drive satisfaction, and satisfaction drives conversion. Since consumers have freedom of choice, they naturally go where they are most satisfied—consumers go where their needs and expectations are met.

# chapter 5

# ATTITUDINAL DATA:

## MEASURING THE MONA LISA'S SMILE

Books have been written about the Mona Lisa and her smile. While this is not one of them, let's take a moment and consider Leonardo da Vinci's painting.

Many people are intrigued by the nature of the Mona Lisa's smile, and some like to speculate about what she seems to be thinking. View the painting in person and one minute she appears radiant, the next slightly serious. The phenomenon is somewhat disconcerting.

It is also explainable. Our eyes generate mixed signals. Different cells in the retina send data about an object's size, brightness, and location to the visual field of our brain. Sometimes we see a smile; other times different cells take over and we do not see a smile. If we look slightly to one side of the painting we are more likely to see a smile because our peripheral vision takes over and transmits different signals. Then, to make matter worse, occasional random noise in the path from our retina to our cortex determines whether we see her smile or not. (Starting to sound like some of the problems that result from relying on traditional metrics?)

So is the Mona Lisa smiling or not? And what is she thinking?

We all have our opinions. Art historians, scientists, and researchers have spent thousands of hours analyzing the question. But no one knows... because we can't ask her or da Vinci. Can we really know what she is thinking?

We can't.

Fortunately, we *can* ask customers what they are thinking. In fact we *must* ask customers what they are thinking. Managing forward means finding and inserting the missing piece—customer satisfaction—into our own measurement puzzles.

Customer satisfaction occurs when you meet a customer's real needs and expectations. Deliver what customers need and expect and they are satisfied. Fail to deliver on needs and expectations and customers are not satisfied.

Know what your customers want. Know what your customers expect. Deliver consistently and reliably, no matter how basic or how extensive and refined. That is customer satisfaction.

## Understanding Expectations is Important

The key to understanding what customers will do in the future requires measuring more than just satisfaction. To be effective, any business must also measure customer needs and expectations, a critical and often ignored piece of the puzzle.

If I go to McDonald's, I don't expect a gourmet meal. I do expect a certain level of quality and fast service at a relatively low price. Deliver on those expectations and I am satisfied.

If I go Fleming's Steak House my expectations include great service, delicious food, and an amazing atmosphere...very different expectations than what I have for McDonald's. In order for me to be satisfied, higher expectations must be met.

If I go to Costco I expect to pay relatively low prices and in return am more than happy to have a "warehouse" experience, to buy in bulk, and to carry out boxes instead of bags. At Nordstrom, where I expect great service, shopping in a brightly lit, cavernous warehouse and leaving with my purchases stacked in discarded apple juice flats will not cut it.

Deliver on my needs and expectations—no matter how basic or how extensive and refined—and I will be satisfied. Fail to deliver and I will not. A simple premise—but one many businesses often overlook, largely because measuring expectations is difficult unless managers can rely on and trust a rigorous, tested methodology.

You cannot manage what you do not measure...and what you measure will ultimately determine what you do. Measuring customer satisfaction starts with understanding expectations and ends with delivering on those expectations. You may be able to help set customer expectations, but in most cases you will not be so fortunate. Success is based on using an accurate, reliable, and precise method to measure the satisfaction of your customers.

# The Analytics Ecosystem

The key to understanding if your customers are smiling (and why or why not) is to comprehensively measure and operate within what we call the Analytics Ecosystem—a set of data and analysis that allows you to predict the future. The Ecosystem is based on using different types of metrics, methodologies, and tools to make the whole significantly stronger and more robust than its individual parts.

The Ecosystem helps solve a long-standing problem. As we have discussed, most traditional metrics attempt to determine—or at best infer—the success of an experience within a channel by counting events like the number of pages viewed, the number of unique customer visits, the number of items sold, the average order size, the number of first-call resolutions, or the number of subscribers.

But counting is not the same as measuring. Recording, sifting, sorting and displaying data is not the same as generating usable information. I deeply believe in the value of attitudinal metrics that measure and analyze the customer experience, but attitudinal metrics cannot always provide basic data like how many visitors came to your site.

The key is to use best-in-class metrics, working together, to provide a complete picture of your customers, their expectations,

## The Measurement Ecosystem

actions, and needs, and their likely future behaviors. No single tool or measurement can provide all of that information.

Notice each element of the Ecosystem revolves around the customer, since the customer is the most important asset of every company.

Let's look at the fundamental elements of the Ecosystem.

# Behavioral Data

Behavioral tools measure what happened using information like financial, transaction, and clickstream data. Clickstream data creates a record of each user's activity on a website and includes traditional measurements like page views, time on site, shopping cart usage, transactions completed...in short, the events that occurred while a visitor was on a website, from the instant the visitor arrived until the instant the visitor departed.

Behavioral Data is a Key Performance Indicator, a set of backwards-looking tools that measures what already happened. Behavioral data is useful information every company should track but is only one piece of the puzzle.

# Observation and Usability

Observation tools are also behavioral in nature but are based on direct and at times real-time studies; some take place in a consumer's natural environment while others are simulated studies that take place in a lab environment. Some of the most popular and valuable kinds of observational tools are those found in the usability field. Usability is the study of the ease with which people are able to use a particular tool, product or software, and the field of usability has exploded along with the Internet explosion.

There are a few kinds of usability testing that are most commonly used for websites:

**Usability in the Lab.** A user is asked to interact with a website while their actions and sometimes even their eye movements are tracked. This type of testing can provide very specific results for how a single user (or small group of users) interacted with a website. Usability experts can see where the user struggled, where the user lingered, what she could not find and what caught her attention, using those results to suggest improvements for a website that will improve usability and in theory improve the overall customer experience.

The results of a usability lab test are beneficial, but remember usability labs evaluate a single user in a controlled environment performing tasks they were asked to perform—instead of operating in their own environment, doing what they want to do.

**Online Usability Tests or Remote Usability Tests:** Technology is deployed to capture or record a user's web session, allowing analysts to view what in effect is a replay or "movie" of visitor behavior as it occurred. Typically these tests do not observe real users in a real environment who are unaware they are being observed but instead observe recruited users (or people expected to be similar to users) who were asked to participate in the test. The tests allow analysts to view a user's mouse movements, mouse clicks, and other site interactions in a way that points out strengths and weaknesses of the site.

**Session Replays:** This type of observation allows for the most natural environment possible—a user environment where visitors pursue their own objectives, not the objectives of the testers, and can do so in their natural environment. The replays allow analysts to view a user's mouse movements, mouse clicks, and other site interactions as the user goes about their business unaware of observation.

**Usability Audits or Heuristic Reviews:** Reviews performed by skilled web navigation specialists who evaluate a website using a range of criteria including site architecture and navigation, user friendliness, page design and layout, functionality, and shopping cart and checkout design. These reviews can be costly when applied to an entire site, but by choosing to focus on specific problem areas, a usability audit on the customer experience of just one element of a site can be performed.

Observation and usability tests, however they are performed, allow analysis usually performed at an aggregate or segment level to be brought down to the level of the individual experience. These observations show what already happened.

# Customer Satisfaction

Measuring satisfaction is based on understanding and measuring attitudes, perceptions, expectations, and intentions. We know, not only intuitively but also from empirical research, that satisfied customers become loyal, long-term customers more likely to make recommendations. Dissatisfied customers go elsewhere when they have the opportunity and may provide negative word of mouth by sharing their poor experiences with others. Customer satisfaction not only helps us measure success today but also provides a leading indicator of what users and customers will do in the future.

Satisfaction, measured correctly, is a Key Success Indicator rather than a Key Performance Indicator because it measures success today and **predicts what will happen in the future.** Satisfaction is proactive and predictive rather than reactive and backwards looking.

At the same time, if you use customer satisfaction analytics alone without a proper integration with the rest of the Ecosystem, you miss data that helps develop a forward-looking action plan.

For example, customer experience analytics may indicate that although customers complain about prices, the best way to engender future loyalty, sales, and recommendations is to improve navigation. Learning you do not have to lower prices is great news, but now that you know navigation must be addressed, how do you fix site navigation problems? Behavioral tools and usability audits can provide the right prescription for future success, but only after the proper issues have been identified by customer experience analytics.

# Feedback

Providing a mechanism for your consumers to give feedback is smart. And when customers provide feedback, listening to that feedback is a no-brainer. Still, we must be cautious in how we use the information customers provide. The difference between feedback and customer experience analytics is that feedback is opt-in (people come to you to tell you what they think) while good customer experience analytics randomly intercept users to create a representative sample of your entire customer base.

Feedback is typically non-representative. Some customers seek out feedback mechanisms and provide feedback; others do not. We typically see a high percentage of feedback that is extremely negative, a much smaller percentage that is extremely positive...and almost no feedback that represents the majority of a company's customer base, the middle ground.

If you only listen to feedback you could completely ignore the silent majority.

Listen to feedback, but do not react to only the squeakiest wheels on the far ends of your customer spectrum. Decide where to allocate resources by determining which improvements will make the biggest impact on your business—which does not always mean fixing what the most people complain about the loudest.

Another problem with feedback is that feedback is reactive. It is easier to react to complaints than it is to proactively identify and measure potential problems. If you wait for feedback to determine where to focus your resources, how many potential customers were lost because their needs were not met—and who never provided feedback you could have acted upon?

Remember, feedback is not inherently bad—in fact any voice of customer information is good—but feedback is reactive. To succeed you must be proactive.

## Putting the Pieces Together

Behavioral data can track what dissatisfied users did. Observational data and session replays can help identify exactly how dissatisfied users interacted with a site. Feedback provides a mechanism for customers who have something to say and provides another source of voice of customer.

Customer experience data identifies opportunities to proactively identify areas for improvement, insuring you can focus on the best ways to improve customer satisfaction.

While the Ecosystem is by its nature input- and output-driven, the process does not stop when customer satisfaction is measured. The Analytics Ecosystem, like any other ecosystem, continually evolves and constantly renews. Changes in each area can affect results in other areas. Correct those problems and satisfaction will increase—and so will financial performance.

In the multichannel world, each channel provides greater value than just the transactions, revenue, or usage of that channel alone; understanding customer needs by applying the

## The Measurement Ecosystem

science of satisfaction to customer experience measurement can improve the value delivered and as a result create more loyal customers and higher long-term revenue.

The Analytics Ecosystem lets you know whether your customers, like the Mona Lisa, are smiling—and more importantly, why.

Credible, reliable, accurate, and precise data, collected using a scientific methodology, uses key performance indicators to create real intelligence—and allows businesses to identify key success indicators and take specific actions that predict future outcomes.

It all starts with useful measurements... driven by a proven methodology. For that discussion let's turn to Dr. Claes Fornell, the creator of the ACSI. Claes has studied the relationship between customer satisfaction and macro- and micro-economic growth for more than thirty-five years at universities around the world including the University of Michigan, Duke University, University of California at Berkeley, INSEAD, the Stockholm School of Economics, and the Helsinki School of Economics.

# chapter 6

# THE AMERICAN CUSTOMER SATISFACTION INDEX

By Claes Fornell
Founder of the American Customer Satisfaction Index
Author of *The Satisfied Customer*

All business books, in one way or another, are about predicting the future, including this one (and my own.) All management decisions and all investment decisions are about relating today to the future: how to influence the future, how to predict it, how to benefit from it, how to defend against it, or how to adapt to it. The truth is that empirical evidence isn't enough—we cannot use what we see and what we observe customers do to make accurate predictions about what they will do in the future or about what will happen to the future of our businesses. Some form of understanding about the forces that shape future events is needed. And, sometimes, a valuable prediction depends on seeing what others don't see—or the opposite to what appears to be true. Here is where value is created and where fortunes are made.

As a visiting professor at the Stockholm School of Economics in the late 1980s, I was asked to develop a system for the Swedish economy that monitored customer satisfaction on a national level and linked it to economic performance. In Sweden, many companies had difficulty competing on price and needed to achieve a better balance between the quantity and quality of their output. That was the logic behind the Swedish Customer Satisfaction Barometer (SCSB): to complement measures of price and quantity with something that would also tell us about quality from the perspective of the consumers of various products and services.

In 1994, similar reasoning led to the adaptation of the Swedish system to the United States, creating the American economy's first national measure of customer satisfaction, the American Customer Satisfaction Index (ACSI).

While much of my research has been related to the macro economy, my work has developed into a strong interest in customers' relationship with individual firms. The good news is that the ACSI has been shown to predict future success at both the macro-economic level and at the company level. The ACSI can provide guidance about the economy as a whole and can also provide guidance to organizations, both public and private, that want to improve outcomes.

## About the ACSI

Since 1994, the American Customer Satisfaction Index (ACSI) has measured almost half of the U.S. economy, including more than two hundred individual companies (online and offline) and more than one hundred federal and local government agencies (offline and online).

Here's how it works. Each year the ACSI interviews more than 80,000 Americans and asks about their satisfaction with the goods and services they have consumed. Respondents are screened to cover a wide range of online and offline consumer products and services in more than forty-five industries such as airlines, apparel, appliances, automobiles, banks and credit unions, cable and satellite television, computers, food manufacturing, insurance, restaurants, retail, utilities, local and national government agencies, and more.

The data resulting from these tens of thousands of customer interviews is then honed and refined using the ACSI statistical engine, a latent-variable, multi-equation econometric model that is essential for turning raw data into a meaningful and useful metric that companies can actually use. The statistical engine is a crucial piece of making this data accurate, precise, and actionable. Raw customer satisfaction scores developed without this kind of cause-and-effect statistical modeling will not be useful as a measure of satisfaction or as a predictor of future behavior.

After the data is run through the statistical engine, we end up with customer satisfaction scores for companies, industries, and economic sectors, all of which are on a 100-point scale. These scores, along with our analysis, are released to the public monthly in an Index. Academic researchers, corporations, government agencies, market analysts, investors, and industry trade associations use the published data. Anyone can go to the ACSI website (www.theacsi.org) and see historical scores for all of the individual companies, industries, and economic sectors included in the Index.

# The ACSI and Macroeconomics

The national ACSI score has been shown to be predictive of both consumer spending and stock market growth. Why is this true?

Peter Drucker said it best many years ago: "The purpose of business is to create a satisfied customer." This is one of the most fundamental principles upon which a free market depends. Sellers compete for buyers. It is what makes the economy grow and what makes things better. It is the satisfaction of customers that brings financial rewards to a company—from customers and investors alike. Likewise, dissatisfied customers punish sellers by taking their business elsewhere in the future.

At the macro level, consumer satisfaction and household spending are at the hub of a free market. In one way or another, everything else—employment, prices, profits, interest rates, production, and economic growth itself—revolve around consumption. Without it, there would be no incentive to produce (and obviously no employment.) Buyer-seller exchange, or money changing hands, is what gets recorded in the national accounts.

The Gross Domestic Product (GDP), the most commonly used gauge for economic progress, is actually the sum of the value of these exchanges. Personal Consumption Expenditures (PCE), or in simpler terms, consumer spending, makes up more than two-thirds of GDP by itself—more than $11 trillion per year. If consumers reduced their spending by as little as 1% to 2% the economy would rapidly head towards recession. If they increase spending, even if by little more than a percentage or two, the effect would be the opposite. No other category or group of decision makers has comparable economic power or influence.

Therefore, consumer satisfaction is the standard for economic growth.

Accordingly, it makes intuitive sense that an accurate, precise measure of customer satisfaction would be predictive of GDP and

PCE growth. Luckily, we do not have to rely on intuition; we can rely on data, science, and measurement over many, many years.

The figure below illustrates the relationship between ACSI and PCE growth.

### Changes in Consumer Spending (PCE) and ACSI (lagged one quarter)

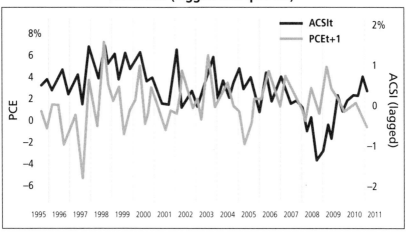

*Source:* www.theacsi.org

# The ACSI and Future Financial Performance

Although the ACSI does not always predict GDP and consumer spending, it usually does a good job of forecasting. Nevertheless, most people are more interested in what this means for their jobs, their companies, and their own investments.

Regardless of how we analyze data or the time periods we assess, we have consistently found a strong and significant relationship between customer satisfaction and a company's future financial performance.

How significant?

The "equity elasticity" averages 4.6%. That means every 1% improvement in customer satisfaction relates to a 4.6% increase in market equity value. Keep in mind this estimate is an average across all companies; some companies have a higher elasticity while others see a weaker relationship. And the research model has somewhat limited cause and effect properties. Yet 4.6% equity elasticity is a dramatic result—and is statistically significant.

Another finding is also interesting. The higher the level of customer satisfaction, the less a company's liabilities reduces its market value. In other words, a company with high customer satisfaction is able to take on more debt than a company with less satisfied customers without adversely affecting its stock price.

But the most remarkable of all our results is the fact that it is possible to create a stock portfolio that consistently does what most mutual funds and hedge funds do not—to consistently beat the market.

Investments in customer satisfaction pay off well in both up and down markets. When the broader stock market rises, the stock prices of many firms with relatively high customer satisfaction scores rise more rapidly. When the stock market falls, the firms with high customer satisfaction fall less. Over time companies with high customer satisfaction scores outperform their competitors—and the market.

Again, it makes intuitive sense that satisfied customers reduce business risk. The customer base is more dependable and less volatile. Satisfied customers are reluctant to "leave" and more likely to buy more. We now have twelve years of data as evidence.

Since 2000s stock portfolio of strong customer satisfaction companies has consistently outperformed, each and every year, the S&P 500.

**Annual Returns, April 11, 2000 – July 21, 2011**

Source: The ACSI, LLC

If you had invested $1 in April of 2000 in this type of portfolio (firms with high satisfaction), you would now have $433, whereas if you had invested that same dollar in the S&P 500 (presumably firms with average customer satisfaction) you would now have just under $90; still an increase, but not nearly as dramatic an increase. During the recession, firms with high customer satisfaction dropped a lot less in value than the market in general (see chart on next page for the value of $1 Invested April 11, 2000 through July 21, 2011)

A word of caution: these results hinge upon the quality of customer satisfaction measurement. Too many companies use primitive systems for their measurement, ignoring scientifically established protocols for minimizing error variance and maximizing predictive powers. Measurement technology often seems to be worse in information/technology firms, a situation that seems counter-intuitive. There is a definite relationship

**Annual Returns, April 11,2000 – July 21, 2011**

Source: The ACSI, LLC

between satisfied customers and the flow of investment capital, but if measurements are poor the relationship is harder
to find. However, as more companies turn to more powerful
measurement tools, the speed at which those companies will
be rewarded will increase.

The ACSI has been used for almost twenty years to measure the health and success of American companies, online and
offline. So how do we apply a scientific, academic principle
used by many countries to individual organizations? We do it
through technology.

# What the Technology Brings

The application of ACSI technology for businesses makes many
things possible. Some of these may sound almost magical to the
layman. We can measure what we can't see, we can put these

unobservables into cause-and-effect systems, we can separate the relevant from the trivial, the signal from the noise, we can generalize from a small sample to a target population, and we can infer what someone's experience may be without asking about it.

This sounds more like Quantum Mechanics than Newtonian Physics. And, it is. Whether we deal with super string theory or "consumer experience" direct observation is inaccessible, meaning depends on context, and it is the statistical behavior of systems that is of concern.

For those who want to know, these types of systems go under the label "Unobservable Variable Structural Equations Systems" and have their roots in the intersection of econometrics, psychometrics, biometrics, chemometrics, computer science, statistics, and mathematics. While this may sound complicated, the system itself is straightforward to implement and is not intrusive. For example, all that is needed to use a website to measure the customer experience is a small piece of JavaScript inserted into the site's HTML.

Now, what does this mean and what can we do with it?

Take the measurement of "experience," or of "satisfaction" for that matter. Instead of relying on the answer to a single question as in traditional surveys, several questions are used—the responses to which are then calibrated with respect to the context in which they belong and according to purpose.

For a website, the drivers or elements of satisfaction are things like navigation, content, site functionality, or a host of other elements that contribute to a user's satisfaction and that have been tested and proven as causal in our model.

The future behaviors a company wants to elicit could be anything from making customers more likely to buy, to return, to open an account, to recommend the company or its products and services, or to join a loyalty program.

The ACSI provides a causal model showing that if you increase satisfaction, you increase likely future behaviors. The technology then shows exactly which elements of a user experience need to be improved in order to impact satisfaction. In this way, companies can use the ACSI to manage their business based on likely future results.

By using the Internet, we can get less costly samples and sometimes a more representative respondent pool. Managers and executives can look at what future behaviors they want to drive, step back to look at increasing satisfaction, and step back again to see which specific drivers will have the greatest impact on satisfaction.

In short, combining the ACSI technology with Internet speed provides a powerful tool for making Internet business better and more efficient. It's a natural fit.

The ACSI applies to just about any industry, including retail, consumer products, healthcare services, financial services, pharmaceuticals, travel services, media and entertainment, telecommunications, B2B and manufacturing, and non-profit and community associations as well as government agencies. It goes back to the fundamental truths that underlie the ACSI methodology and make it work: the extent to which buyers financially reward sellers that satisfy them and punish those that don't is fundamental to how free markets operate. A well-functioning market allocates resources, including capital, to create the greatest possible consumer satisfaction, as efficiently as possible. The discontent buyer will not remain a customer unless there is nowhere else to go, or it is too expensive to get there. In a competitive marketplace that offers meaningful consumer choice, firms that do well by their customers are rewarded by repeat business, lower price elasticity, higher reservation prices, more cross-selling opportunities, greater marketing efficiency and a host of other things that usually lead to earnings growth.

Companies win, consumers win, the economy wins...everyone wins.

# chapter 7

# HOW DOES CUSTOMER SATISFACTION PREDICT THE FUTURE?

L et's expand on Claes' thoughts regarding ways to apply technology to measure the customer experience and predict the future.

In the previous chapter, Claes shared the fundamental model shown below. The model applies to all industries and all touch points and has been used to successfully manage businesses forward by measuring the customer experience across all channels across thousands of companies around the world. For our purposes, we will apply the model in terms of the online channel.

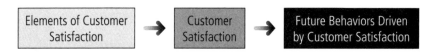

It may help to think of the web experience in simple terms. Your visitors experience many different elements of your website as they navigate. Depending on your industry and the nature of your site, those elements might include:

> Content

> Functionality

> Search

> Look and feel

> Navigation

> Site performance

> Transparency

> Advertising

> Merchandise

> Ordering Process

> Privacy

As a result of that experience (or as a result of the combination of a user's experience of some or all of those elements), customers are satisfied with their visit (or not) based on their intentions and expectations. That is the next step in the customer satisfaction puzzle:

Extensive research proves that increasing customer satisfaction leads to the kinds of future behaviors we want from our customers. Again, the future behaviors to measure and track depend on your industry.

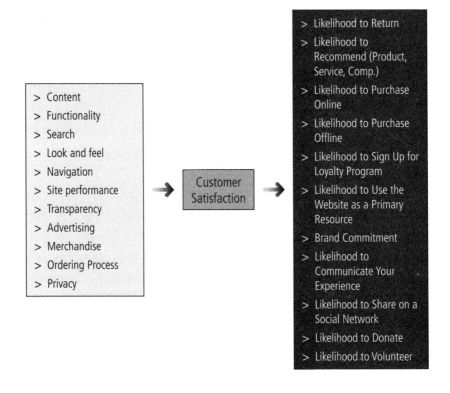

Our goal is to truly understand the totality of the customer experience. That is why all elements of the satisfaction measurement model provide value and help businesses manage forward. In every customer experience, success is defined from your customer's perspective. Did you meet their needs and exceed their expectations? In short, were your customers satisfied?

Let's take a hypothetical example. Say you run the online division of a huge national insurance company. Two critical customer behaviors contribute to bottom line success for your company, above all others:

1. The customers' likelihood to use the website as a primary channel to receive insurance quotes and service their account, saving you millions of dollars annually in call center costs, and

2. The customer's likelihood to purchase a policy on your website.

You implement a customer satisfaction model on your website. The model shows that to improve these two future behaviors, you must improve satisfaction.

But *how* do you improve satisfaction? The model will show which element of your website will have the greatest impact on satisfaction.

That element may not be the lowest-scoring element. As mentioned earlier, customers always complain about prices, and many of our clients find price is their lowest-scoring element. Even so—and this is very often the case—other elements like site navigation or site functionality should be the highest priority.

For our imaginary insurance company, overall site navigation does in fact turn out to be the biggest issue impacting satisfaction. Usability audits and other observational methods can then be used to determine specific navigation issues. If the insurance company improves navigation they improve satisfaction. If the insurance company improves satisfaction they increase a customer's likelihood to use the website instead of the call center, and they increase the number of policies purchased online.

The results are direct, make a real bottom-line impact, and are easy to measure and quantify.

Here is another example showing how the methodology works, underscoring the perils of relying solely on opt-in feedback. We worked with a retailer whose site performance monitoring tools showed their site performance was declining. In addition, they had received a few complaints regarding the website's page load time. The retailer's technology team suggested a $3M capital improvement to improve their back-end systems and significantly improve page load performance.

We applied the ACSI methodology to measure customer experiences on the website. Our methodology indicated that improved product descriptions would increase sales far more significantly than improved page load times. The customer hired a freelance copywriter to improve product descriptions and saw online sales increase by 18% that year—without making any other changes.

And they never spent a dime on site performance.

## Customer Satisfaction in the Ecosystem

Customer satisfaction can help you drill deep and accurately diagnose your customers' experiences, especially when used in conjunction with behavioral and observational information.

The way you gather data in each channel and how that data fits into the Ecosystem is different, but the role the Ecosystem plays in helping you turn that data into intelligence is the same. In the bricks-and-mortar retail environment, the behavioral analytics used include sales, inventory turns, returns, foot traffic, conversions, and others. In the web environment the behavioral analytics used include sales, conversions, page visits, unique visitors, etc.

In both channels, behavioral metrics tell what people have done, data that is an important part of the Ecosystem and an important way to measure the success of customer experiences. But using components of the Ecosystem incorrectly can lead to poor assumptions, to taking the wrong actions, and even to failure.

For example, say you are the head of marketing for Ford Motor Company. You decide to run a television commercial. Your ultimate goal is obviously to sell more cars, but your more immediate goal is to drive visits to dealerships and to your website.

How will you know if your television commercial drives more traffic to the Ford website? The problem in answering that question lies in the data available.

Some visitors arrive by typing the URL www.ford.com. Others search using a term like "Ford" and click on the resulting link in the natural search results. Others click a sponsored link. More visitors arrive via banner ads you place on a variety of sites. Still others arrive by clicking links in news items, automobile reviews, or press releases you issue. The possibility for inbound links is endless when your goal is to market a huge global corporation through as many channels as possible.

What drove your visitors? Was it the television commercial? Was it a favorable review in *Motor Trend* magazine? Was it a photo they saw of a celebrity driving a Ford? Gauging the impact of a single influencing item in an environment where multiple potential influencers exist can be incredibly difficult. Unfortunately, we do not live in a lab environment where we can evaluate one new potential influencer at a time.

How *can* you distinguish and differentiate? One easy answer is to assume visitors who clicked on a sponsored link in Google did not arrive as result of your television commercial...but still, can you really be sure? Possibly the commercial created greater overall brand awareness and that interest resulted in the user going to Google, searching for the car in the ad, and clicking the sponsored link. Behavioral data alone cannot answer the question of the TV ad's influence on site traffic.

While there are certainly old-fashioned ways to measure the impact of TV ads, like using panels, those methods have not kept pace with the growth of the Internet as a marketing, information, and commerce channel. Using the Analytics Ecosystem we can use our attitudinal tools (like customer satisfaction and voice of customer measurement) to know what influenced visitors to visit the site, to know if based on expectations set by the ad the site met their expectations, to know if they were satisfied with their experience, and to know whether they are likely to visit a dealership or to consider buying a Ford as a result of their experience.

Using the Analytics Ecosystem allows you to gain intelligence previously unavailable and make decisions that allow you to manage your business forward.

That is why behavioral analytics, deployed on their own, can be misleading. While you are certainly able to count, you are unable to turn data into intelligence—and the ability to measure success is lost.

# Measuring Customer Satisfaction: A Broader Impact

Blending behavioral data with attitudinal data ensures customer satisfaction is no longer the missing piece of a comprehensive measurement puzzle.

Measurements and methodologies must be accurate and precise in order to provide actionable data—data and intelligence that is good not only for your business but for business and society as a whole.

Claes embraces a philosophy that I wholeheartedly agree with. Companies that make customer satisfaction a true priority are actually good for humanity.

Sound like overreaching?

Good companies become great companies and are rewarded for their efforts—and their customers benefit. Poor companies are, for want of a better word, punished—and their customers seek better options. In fact those companies are often punished twice, first by customers defecting, which leads to poor financial performance, and then by the capital markets that punish them as a result of poor financial performance.

When companies provide products and services that satisfy a customer, the customer is not only more satisfied but also receives greater overall value and a better life experience. The products we use are more satisfying and the services we receive are more satisfying. Applications work better. Websites work better. Value is magnified.

When you truly measure customer satisfaction and turn data into intelligence, you make the right decisions that lead to success—for you, for your customers, for everyone.

Granted, we are not creating world peace through customer satisfaction, but it does feel close enough that doing this work has been meaningful and fulfilling to myself and my colleagues for many years.

So how do we get to world peace—or at least to a truly satisfied customer? Before we discuss measurement best practices, let's take a closer look at a few mistakes we have all made in our quest for actionable data and meaningful customer intelligence.

# chapter 8

# MEASURING WELL IS *HARD*

**W**e all need a methodology. But simply *having* a methodology does not guarantee success.

What is a methodology? A methodology is often just a system of measurements accompanied by an acronym. Nowhere is it said a methodology must to be accurate, precise or reliable. There are "methodologies" on the market today with margin of error rates in the double digits, but I have no doubt the people using them still have confidence in those methodologies.

A truly useful methodology is accurate, precise, and reliable. Otherwise the methodology is garbage in, garbage out. Inaccurate and imprecise methodologies lead to poor decisions—and to a false sense of confidence in those decisions. We will look at how to effectively evaluate a methodology in detail in Chapter 12, but first let's take a brief look at some of the basic measurement mistakes many companies make.

# Common Measurement Mistakes

## Common Measurement Mistake #1: Drawing conclusions from incomplete information.

Every day your business generates a tremendous amount of data—but that data may not tell the full story. Say your analytics show visitors spend a relatively high amount of time on a particular page. Is that page great—or is it problematic? Possibly visitors love the content. Or they may be getting stuck due to a problem on the page.

Possibly your call center statistics show average call time has decreased. Is a decrease in average call time good news or bad news? When calls end more quickly, costs go down, but have you actually satisfied callers or left them disgruntled, dissatisfied, and on their way to your competition? Without additional information to help better evaluate the data, you simply cannot know.

Never draw conclusions from any statistical analysis that does not tell the whole story.

## Common Measurement Mistake #2: Failing to look forward.

Every company seeks to look forward, and measuring customer satisfaction after an activity or transaction is certainly helpful, but what if you also want to better predict the future? Measuring customer satisfaction by itself will not provide the best view forward. Using a complete satisfaction measurement system—including future behaviors and predictive metrics such as likelihood to return to the site or likelihood to purchase again—generates leading indicators that complement and illuminate lagging indicators.

## Common Measurement Mistake #3: Assuming a lab is a reasonable substitute.

Usability groups and observation panels are certainly useful and have their place; the problem is the sample sizes are small and the testing takes place in a controlled environment. Say you bring people into a lab and tell them what you want them to do. Does that small group of eight participants represent your broader audience? Does measuring and observing them when they do what *we* tell them to do provide the same results as real users who do what *they* want to do? Observation is helpful, but applying science to the voice of customer and measuring the customer experience through the lens of customer satisfaction is critical to success.

## Common Measurement Mistake #4: Forgetting the real experts are your customers.

Experts, like usability groups, have their place. But who knows customer intentions, customer needs, and customer attitudes better than actual customers? When you really want to know, go to the source. It takes more time and work, but the results are much more valuable. I cannot say how many times I have been in meetings with analysts and experts who swear that a new site navigation system will solve every problem on a particular website. (Oddly enough, there often is money to be made if the analysts are hired to develop that new navigation system. Unfortunately solutions are often based on what the expert can provide rather than what the customer needs.) Meanwhile, what customers want are more product varieties to choose from. Experts and consultants certainly have their place, but their advice and recommendations must be driven by customer needs as much if not more than by organizational needs.

## Common Measurement Mistake #5: Confusing causation and correlation.

Failing to understand the difference between correlation and causation, and how those concepts should be applied, is a major problem that often leads companies to make major strategic mistakes.

Here is a classic example of the difference in correlation and causation. Let's say I plan to write a white paper on public safety. I conduct research and determine the more firefighters that fight a fire, the more damage the fire causes.

I am surprised. That cannot make sense—possibly my sample size is too small? I research other towns and get the same results. I conduct sufficient research to ensure my results are statistically valid. Even accounting for an appropriate margin of error, clearly more firefighters equals more fire damage.

If I take my results at face value, I might decide that dramatically reducing the number of firefighters will decrease the amount of damage caused by fires. That decision would also be a huge mistake.

Why? I mistook correlation for causation.

The number of firefighters fighting a fire does indeed *correlate* with the amount of damaged caused by the fire. The reason is simple. The bigger the fire, the more firefighters needed to fight the fire. The bigger the fire, the more damage caused by the fire. Originally we correlated two data points—more damage and more firefighters—when in fact both were caused by a third element, bigger fires.

While the above is a simple example, it is often easy to use intuition, gut feel, or fuzzy logic to distinguish between causation and correlation. Confusion between correlation and causation often occurs in science, health, and even sports, and is seen in virtually every media report regarding most new research findings.

In theory, causation and correlation are easy to distinguish. Correlation exists when there is a relationship between two variables (events or actions). Causation exists when one event is the direct result of another event. A prime example is that smoking can cause lung cancer.

The same action or occurrence can also *correlate* with another occurrence; smoking is correlated with alcohol abuse. One action that directly causes another action is causation. But simply because two actions *occur* together in no way indicates one action *causes* the other action.

Here's another example. Towns with higher ice cream sales have higher drowning rates. Clearly ice cream does not cause drowning. The two facts are correlated but not causal. The causal factor is weather. In towns with higher temperatures, more ice cream is sold, more people swim...and more people drown. A town that attempts to prevent drowning by restricting ice cream sales will obviously miss the mark.

One more example: for years eating a healthy breakfast has been shown to correlate with success in school. Children who eat breakfast tend to perform better in school than those who do not eat breakfast. By extension that indicates eating breakfast helps us to be better learners.

Not so fast. Children who do not eat breakfast also tend to have higher absentee rates. Failing to attend school has a direct effect on scholastic performance. Researchers took their study a step farther and determined the only causal factor present was that eating breakfast helped *undernourished* children perform better in school. In and of itself, eating breakfast was not a causal factor in scholastic performance, regardless of how linking those two items seems to make intuitive sense.

Now let's look at correlation and causation in business terms.

Say you sell clothing offline and online. One of the shirts you sell is available in a variety of colors. In an offline environment shoppers can easily see the different colors in person; online is a different story. You decide to add an application to your site allowing visitors to change the color of the image of a particular shirt instead of simply viewing a set of color swatches; that way potential customers can see the difference on a virtual product. Sales go up and conversion rates go up. (In fact, one of our clients enjoyed the same results when they made a similar change to their website.)

In the above example, the change you made correlates to higher sales and conversions and also is a causal factor. If you made no other changes to your site, ran no promotions, and did not market differently, you can safely determine your change was a direct—and positive—causal factor.

What if you made that change but also ran a special on the shirts? You would need to dig deeper to determine the relative effects of those two different actions on sales and conversion rates. Was it the new application on your website that increased sales, or did sales increase due to the special?

To generate truly meaningful data you must know a lot more about your customers—where they came from, why they visited your site, what they did while on your site, etc.—before you can determine which actions correlate and which are truly causal factors.

## Common Measurement Mistake #6: Confusing feedback and measurement.

Feedback is not measurement. Feedback does provide depth and meaning, though. Once you have data you can use feedback to add context, color, and possibly gain a deeper understanding of the data. After you identify a problem you can hone in on that problem by using feedback to let you move from identifying an area of focus to identifying specific actions.

That is why you should always listen. In fact the more open feedback paths you can create, the better. But simply receiving feedback via the opt-in approach is in no way sufficient.

Examples of opt-in feedback include a customer who clicks a link and completes a feedback form; a customer who calls your 800-number to complain; a customer who writes a letter (does anyone still get letters?); or a customer who sends an email to the CEO. Those are examples of opt-in feedback; in essence the customer took the initiative to provide feedback. Feedback was not required so feedback was voluntary.

Opt-in feedback is valuable, but it is not a measurement.

The problem with opt-in feedback is its inherent bias towards the squeaky wheel. People who like you seldom give you feedback. People who hate you often will. (I know "hate" is a strong word, but opt-in feedback is often delivered in very strong words.)

The challenge where opt-in feedback is concerned is to determine if a limited number of opinions are truly representative of a larger group. A customer who does not like your product and explains why provides interesting feedback, but absent of other data that feedback should not cause you to make wholesale product changes. On the other end of the spectrum, some customers who love your products tend to share those feelings but many will not. They simply keep buying. What is lost is the quiet majority, all the consumers who are not at either end of the spectrum but instead sit in the middle—and are often least likely to seek out and provide feedback.

It is difficult to make sense of general and extreme end-of-spectrum feedback. But, if a customer says she tried to download a white paper and your online application failed, her feedback provides specific information you can wrap your arms around. Plus you get the opportunity to respond directly to her concerns and hopefully turn a problem into a positive, even memorable solution.

Depending on the tools you use, testing, monitoring, or clickstream data may or may not identify the problem. Still, when you receive feedback about a particular issue you do receive information you can use to make positive changes that can directly improve customer satisfaction.

The beauty of opt-in feedback is that customers can use their own words, allowing you to learn about issues or problems a poorly designed survey may not identify. (You can achieve a similar result by using random sampling that allows participants to answer open-ended questions.)

So make it easy for customers to provide feedback, but never try to use opt-in feedback as a measurement or critical metric. Opt-in feedback is only information, not intelligence. Opt-in feedback provides reactive information; measurement provides proactive intelligence.

## Common Measurement Mistake #7: Gaming the system.

Unfortunately, many feedback and measurement systems create bias and inaccuracy. How? Ask the wrong people, bias their decisions, or give them incentives for participation. Measuring correctly means creating as little measurement bias as possible while generating as little measurement noise as possible.

Try to avoid incenting people to complete surveys, especially when there is no need. Never ask for personal data; some customers will decline to participate if only for privacy or confidentiality concerns.

Also never measure with the intent to prove a point. Unfortunately, research run by internal staff can often contain some amount of built-in bias. As employees we may, however unintentionally, create customer measurements to prove our opinions are correct or support our theories, but to what end?

Customer measurements must measure from the customers' perspective and through the customers' eyes, not through a lens of preconceived views.

## Common Measurement Mistake #8: Sampling problems.

Sampling works well when sampling is done correctly. Sample selection and sample size are critical to creating a credible, reliable, accurate, precise, and predictive methodology. Sampling is a science in and of itself. We need samples representative of the larger population that are randomly selected.

## Common Measurement Mistake #9: Faulty math.

Taking a binary approach to measuring satisfaction—in effect, asking whether I *am* or *am not* satisfied—leads to a very simplistic and inaccurate measurement.

Intelligence is not binary. People are not just smart or stupid. People are not just tall or short. Customers are not just satisfied or dissatisfied. "Yes" and "no" do not accurately explain or define levels or nuances of customer satisfaction. The *degree* of satisfaction is what determines the customer's level of loyalty and positive word of mouth.

Claiming 97% of your customers are satisfied certainly makes for a catchy marketing slogan but is far from a metric you can use to manage your business forward.

If you cannot trust and use the results, why do the research?

## Common Measurement Mistake #10: Measurement by proxy.

Trying to measure customer satisfaction by measuring a behavior like task completion is commonly referred to as "measurement by proxy." When measuring by proxy there may at times be a correlation between task completion and satisfaction, but all too often that is not the case.

The key is to identify causation. How many times have you completed a particular task ... but still left dissatisfied and vowing never to do business with the company again?

The same phenomenon occurs if you attempt to measure customer loyalty by evaluating customer recommendations or by the likelihood customers will make a recommendation. Either way the end result is measurement by proxy; you attempt to determine one attitude or intention by measuring another. Doing so can create significant measurement noise and render your measurements useless in the process.

To highlight the point, let's look more closely at task completion.

Some measurement tools measure task completion as a proxy for measuring customer satisfaction. The underlying theory assumes that when a customer completes a task the customer must therefore be satisfied.

That theory falls apart if a software update takes ten minutes to download and another twenty minutes of struggle and frustration to install. The customer may have completed the task but is far from satisfied and may never return. Worse, the customer may say negative things to others and generate negative word of mouth.

Here's another example. Say you visit a store to find a special tie for a party you will attend tonight. You find the tie, but locating an employee to ring up your purchase is a challenge. After ten minutes of searching you find a salesperson. He is less than friendly, bordering on rude. Do you still buy the tie? Yes, because you don't have time to go elsewhere ... but as you leave the store you vow never to return.

At the party you receive a nice compliment on the tie (your shopping experience was awful but your sartorial judgment is impeccable) and you tell the story about the terrible service you received, compounding the impact of your bad experience by generating negative word of mouth.

Task completion only measures—no surprise—whether a task was completed. Task completion does not measure satisfaction and does not measure future intentions. Task completion is a poor stand-in for customer satisfaction, but since task completion is data that can be gathered fairly easily many businesses and even experts yield to temptation and use task completion as a proxy for customer satisfaction.

Using proxies is easy. Measuring well is hard. The result of using proxies is measurement and management by inference rather than management based on real data, real intelligence, and real knowledge.

Take the practice of measuring loyalty based on recommendations. McDonald's customers are satisfied—otherwise McDonald's would not enjoy its current market share—but McDonald's customers also do not tend to be particularly vocal. People who love Big Macs may not be particularly likely to recommend Big Macs to others.

In large part that tendency is due to the nature of the product and to the way people wish to be perceived. (In-N-Out Burger customers, on the other hand, tend to be much more vocal about their love of the franchise.)

Some people may be likely to recommend Whole Foods, especially if they wish to be perceived as health- and environmentally-conscious. On the other hand, some may not be as likely to recommend the Wal-Mart grocery department to their friends even though they are incredibly loyal Wal-Mart customers. A number of products—deodorants, toilet paper, dandruff shampoos, etc.—fall into this "recommendation paradigm." We tend not to share our dirty laundry or our less-than-flattering secrets.

Personality can also play a major role in whether we recommend products or services. Many highly loyal customers simply do not recommend products or companies to others.

Perceived perception also can greatly influence whether you are likely to recommend, but perception does not have the same impact on customer loyalty. Say you find great clothing at a discount retailer. Some may recommend the discount retailer to others, but many will not because they prefer that others assume they buy their clothing from high-end retailers. The influence of perception does not impact their level of loyalty but does impact their likelihood to recommend.

Finding ways to get customers to recommend your business, and measuring their likelihood to recommend your business, is smart business and often generates substantial revenue. But never use recommendation as a proxy for satisfaction or loyalty. Never use satisfaction as a proxy for recommendation or for loyalty.

And while it should go without saying, never use loyalty as a proxy for satisfaction or recommendation.

If you decide to measure recommendations then by all means measure recommendations—but never try to infer loyalty in the process. The relationship between recommendations and loyalty is not causal, even if at times the relationship does show correlation.

Research from universities and corporations around the world consistently proves that satisfaction is causal and is a key driver of recommendations and of customer loyalty.

## Common Measuring Mistake #11:
## Keep it simple—too simple.

The "keep it simple" approach does not work for measuring customer satisfaction (or, really, for measuring anything regarding customer attitudes and behaviors.)

Customers are complex individuals who make decisions based on a number of criteria, most rational, some less so. Asking three or four questions does not create a usable metric or help to develop actionable intelligence. Still, many companies take this approach and make major strategic decisions—and often compensate their executives—based on a limited and therefore flawed approach to measurement.

Great managers do not make decisions based on hunches or limited data; "directionally accurate" is simply not good enough when our companies and our customers are at stake.

Great managers also pay attention.

# chapter 9

# THE PERILS OF INATTENTION

Some businesses notice, too late, a shift in customer needs. A great example of inattention and a lack of strategic vision is Blockbuster Video.

At one time Blockbuster was arguably the king of the movie and video game rental business. Founded in 1985, Blockbuster experienced phenomenal growth and at one point opened a new store every day. Then strategic missteps and a failure to understand the changing consumer landscape all but doomed the company.

In 1998, Warner Brothers offered Blockbuster, then the studio's single largest source of revenue, a unique opportunity. Warner Brothers proposed the creation of a "rental window." During the rental window, DVDs for certain movies would not be offered for sale through any other channel. In effect Block-buster would enjoy, at the very least, a short-term monopoly on movie consumption. For example, say Blockbuster had "owned" a rental window on the movie *Titanic*; during the window the only way to watch Titanic on DVD would be to rent the movie from Blockbuster. If you wanted to buy the DVD, you would be forced to wait until the rental window had closed.

In return the studio asked for approximately 40% of the rental revenues Blockbuster would earn from DVDs, the same amount the studio received from VHS tape rentals. (Remember, this was when DVDs were first introduced.)

Blockbuster turned Warner Brothers down.

In response, movie studios decided to price DVDs low enough so consumers would consider purchasing DVDs as a viable alternative to renting DVDs. Wal-Mart in particular seized the opportunity. By 2003 the studios made three times the revenue from DVD sales than from VHS sales, and of course VHS sales virtually disappeared as DVD players became ubiquitous in American homes, computers, and cars.

In the space of a few years, Wal-Mart became the movie studios' largest source of revenue—not Blockbuster. Other retailers recognized the opportunity, some even offering movies below wholesale as a loss leader for other products. Blockbuster was forced to compete with extremely low prices, both on rentals and on sales of new movies, but since Blockbuster had few other products to sell, competing on price alone proved deadly. No business can take a loss on one product unless it can sell other products at profit levels sufficient to offset those losses.

To make a bad situation worse, Netflix (and later Redbox, Amazon, and Hulu) emerged as competitors. At one point Blockbuster could have purchased Netflix for approximately $50 million but instead chose to create its own service, the Blockbuster Online network. Netflix differentiated its service by providing DVDs for a monthly fee, which allowed customers to avoid late fees. To try to remain competitive Blockbuster was forced to eliminate its late fees, a profit center that had generated significant incremental revenue.

By 2005 Netflix had over three million subscribers; today there are approximately twelve million subscribers and growing. Netflix also began offering online movies to its ever-expanding customer base, limiting the growth of Blockbuster Online and further eroding Blockbuster's overall market share. As a result, the 4,000-plus Blockbuster locations became a liability instead of a competitive advantage; what was a convenient nearby location suddenly became inconvenient when customers switched to receiving DVDs by mail and watching movies online.

Blockbuster knew it needed to change its business model; that awareness required no special information or intelligence. But instead of assessing a changing landscape to determine what mattered most to customers, Blockbuster stuck to a core value proposition long past the time when that proposition truly created value—both in financial terms and to its customers. Blockbuster viewed the market through its own eyes instead of through the eyes of its customers.

In 2005 Blockbuster stock traded at over $9 per share. In July 2010 the stock fell well below $1 per share and was delisted from the New York Stock Exchange. In September 2010 Blockbuster filed for Chapter 11 bankruptcy protection and today continues to search for a competitive strategy.

## Traditional Media Faces a Similar Challenge

Newspapers are both a conventional and online example of the impact of a changing marketplace and a failure to respond to customer needs.

The newspaper industry was slow to embrace changes to their business model created by the Internet. Most publishers saw the Internet as an afterthought and felt maintaining a web presence was a necessary evil rather than an opportunity. The competition moved quickly, and as more people turned to the web for news—in fact, to the newspapers' own websites—fewer and fewer people paid to read the news in print. Circulation decreased and so did advertising revenues. As advertising revenues dipped, profits vanished and most papers were forced to cut staffing and other costs to stay in business.

A few papers—most notably the *New York Times*, a corporation that has arguably poured the greatest resources into addressing the changing business landscape—established a substantial online presence but have struggled to monetize that presence to generate significant revenues, much less replace revenues lost from decreased advertising on the print side of their business.

Most experts feel the days of large newsrooms and extensive newsgathering organizations are rapidly drawing to an end. Yet consumer consumption of news is at an all-time high; more outlets than ever before—online, of course—exist to disseminate news and information.

What happened? To most consumers, news is now considered to be "free." Because it is easy to read breaking news on any number of websites, the thought of paying for news is now foreign to most people. (Why subscribe to a daily paper when you can read it online for free?) Many major news organizations continue to experiment and struggle with variations of "paid access" to complement online ad revenue.

Still, some online news outlets are successful. For example, the *Huffington Post*, recently acquired by AOL, has shown that online advertising revenue can support a quasi-news organization. Other organizations will follow suit, encouraged by technological advances. Subsequent versions of e-readers like the Kindle or iPad will revolutionize how we consume all types of media, including news, and may encourage consumers to pay for news—as long as the method of delivery creates a com-pelling advantage.

Few consumers are willing to pay for a product unless they find an abundance of perceived value. In a nutshell, that is the Internet challenge—create a real perception of value in a world of Accelerated Darwinism and the Super Consumer.

While news organizations certainly collected data, analyzed web metrics, and worked as hard as possible to find solutions to a changing marketplace, it is easy to argue that most failed to accept the balance of power had shifted to the consumer . . . and failed to listen to what the consumer really wanted. Newspapers possessed a massive amount of information showing consumer news consumption habits were changing but did not turn that information into strategic intelligence. Many tried instead to hang on to a model of the past they knew well.

The clues were there for Blockbuster and the newspapers to hear . . . but they didn't *listen*.

So how do *you* listen? How do you turn data into informa-tion and information into intelligence? Let's look at the problem at a finer level.

First, you do not need expensive technology and a dedi-cated staff in order to collect and analyze data. Even free tools like Google Analytics can generate massive amounts of data. From hits, page views, and click-throughs to retained visitors and visitor segmentation tools, data can be collected in a variety of ways and the results can fill an endless stream of binders.

But, even if you do pay attention, do you truly measure what matters most to your business?

To show you how far afield a flawed measurement tool can take your business, let's take a close look at on one popular tool: Net Promoter Score.

# chapter 10

# SIMPLE IS NOT ALWAYS BEST

Our businesses grow more complex every day. In a busy and complicated business environment we instinctively search for simplicity. Business leaders are naturally drawn to the hope of simplicity and the promise of growth.

A moderately popular management tool that promises simplicity as well as a path to growth is Net Promoter Score (NPS).

My goal is not to criticize NPS, although criticism may certainly appear to be the outcome of the following analysis. Instead my goal is to discuss a management tool in detail so you can understand how easy it is to assume a "metric" has real validity—especially if that metric receives widespread corporate and media attention—and so you will better understand why the Analytics Ecosystem is a vital component in measuring forward.

Let's start with the positives. The adoption of Net Promoter Score has truly been helpful in some ways. NPS has brought more attention to the importance of the customer in growing a business (a focus I always appreciate.) More resources have been allocated to measure the customer's impact. Some companies pay more attention to the customer. NPS has also brought more attention and focus to the power of positive word of mouth as a driver of growth. Finally, NPS has framed a concept in a way that is easy and simple for companies to understand.

Those outcomes are all positive, or at least they can be positive.

Before we look at my concerns with Net Promoter Score, let's take a look at how it works. Companies using NPS ask their customers a single question:

*"On a scale of 0 to 10, with 10 being the highest, how likely are you to recommend our company to a friend or colleague?"*

Based on the response, customers are then categorized into one of three groups:

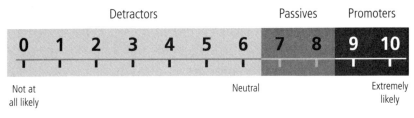

Source: Net Promoter

Subtracting the percentage of Detractors from the percentage of Promoters results in a Net Promoter Score, a score that could theoretically range from –100 to +100.

The theory behind Net Promoter is that knowing how many people will promote your company—or detract from it—is the only metric needed to predict and encourage growth. (The actual tagline is, "The one number you need to grow.")

As an added bonus, along the way companies can also break their addiction to "bad profits." Net Promoter defines bad profits as any profits that come at the expense of frustrating or annoying a customer since those feelings are "detractors" to a business.

The appeal of tracking a simple, single metric is understandable. It sounds simple. It sounds easy. The idea behind the Net Promoter concept makes sense. Word of mouth, whether positive, negative, or nonexistent, is a crucial business metric and should absolutely be measured. NPS sounds, at first glance, great. But as a management tool, NPS just does not work.

How do I know?

I am fortunate to be in a position to look a lot more closely at the validity of NPS as a measurement tool. Since 2001 we have collected more than sixty million online customer satisfaction surveys that measure "likelihood to recommend." In fact, our research precedes the introduction of the NPS concept.

We have also performed a bi-annual survey of the top-grossing online retailers for the last several years, the ForeSee Online Retail Satisfaction Index, a survey that includes additional questions allowing us to measure just how accurate, precise, actionable, and predictive a Net Promoter Score (NPS) really is. In addition, we work with top economists at the University of Michigan and other universities who help us evaluate the science and statistics behind the Net Promoter claims.

Here are a few of the problems we have found with Net Promoter Score. Keep these issues in mind as you evaluate your own measurement tools.

## Accuracy

At first glance a scale of 0 to 10 appears to provide a great deal of accuracy and precision. (Accuracy is to what degree you are correct; precision is to what degree you are exact—more on that in Chapter 12.) Certainly a scale of 0 to 10 appears to provide accuracy and precision. But at closer inspection NPS actually uses a three-point scale, in fact what I like to call a three-point "unbalanced scale." Since values of 0 to 6 are Detractors, 7 and 8 are Passives, and 9 and 10 are Promoters, the scale does not use eleven points. The scale uses three points.

Using the NPS calculation does not result in scores that fall between 0 and 10. There are only three results: Detractors, Passives, and Promoters. The scale is unbalanced. In the real world the difference between a 4 and 5 is the same as the difference between a 6 and 7; each is different by one. Under the NPS scale that is no longer true. There is *no* difference between a 4 and 5, since both are considered to be Detractors, but there *is* a difference between a 6 and 7 because a 6 is a Detractor and a 7 is a Passive.

The scale is unbalanced because the groupings arbitrarily combine real differences into general categories.

# Margin of Error

As a result of the scale used by Net Promoter Score, the margin of error almost always falls well outside the range of statistical confidence. We evaluated published NPS benchmarks and calculated the margin of error. In most cases 60% to 80% of the published results were statistically the same and fell within the margin of error.

In simpler terms, even though two different NPS scores may have been reported as a 40 and 50, when we applied the rules of statistics the numbers were in fact not statistically different.

When we calculate overall customer satisfaction scores for the one hundred top grossing online retailers, we find based on our sample size the margin of error for a customer satisfaction score is +/– 2.6 points. When we assess the Net Promoter score (using the same sample size and confidence level), we find a +/– 10-point margin of error.

Essentially, a Net Promoter Score of 12.5 could actually be anywhere from 2.5 to 22.5—a range so large that it is basically useless.

# Over-simplification

Net Promoter Score asks survey respondents to rate whether they would recommend a company on a scale of 0 to 10. Sounds great...but again those responses are combined into three broad categories:

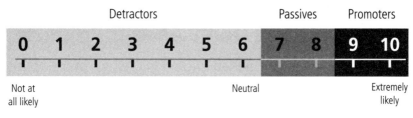

*Source:* Net Promoter

Reducing a ten-point scale to a three-point scale greatly increases the margin of error and eliminates subtle but important differences in customer behavior.

The results from the ForeSee Online Retail Satisfaction Index show that people who rate their "likelihood to recommend" as a 6 are ten times more likely to buy offline than people who score themselves as a 1. More impressively, the 6s are fourteen times more likely to purchase next time than the 1s, and a massive *thirty times* more likely to purchase on the web. Lumping 1s and 6s together defeats the purpose since we lose the ability to differentiate between customers with disparate buying behaviors.

It gets worse. When we looked at the respondents considered to be Promoters (people who scored themselves as 9s or 10s on the NPS scale), we found that people who rated their "likelihood to recommend" as a 10 were 57% more likely to purchase online than those who rated themselves as 9s. The 10s were also 56% more likely to purchase offline and to make a purchase the next time they shopped for similar merchandise.

Create ratings "buckets," and toss out results differentiation, and you are left with no real way to interpret and act on subtleties in customer attitudes and behaviors—attitudes and behaviors that can have a direct and tangible impact on revenues and profitability.

## Detractors Don't *Always* Detract, and Promoters Don't *Always* Promote

Following a hunch, we added two additional questions to our surveys to see if the Net Promoter concept accurately reflects the customer behavior it claims to measure.

Our initial assumption was that people decide to recommend or not to recommend a product or company for a number of different reasons. Some will only recommend items that make them feel trendy, like the latest smart phone. Others will not recommend a product or service no matter how much they love it. And some products no one will recommend because those products are too personal. (Can you imagine recommending your favorite brand of toilet paper to a friend?)

In fact, NPS does not measure how likely a consumer is to say something negative at all. NPS only purports to measure a customer's likelihood of saying something positive.

When we ran the next ForeSee Online Retail Satisfaction Index (and have ever since), we asked three questions, including the Net Promoter question:

> > *How likely are you to recommend this website?* (The Net Promoter question.)

> *How likely would you be to communicate your experi-
> ence with this website to other people?*

> *Assuming you communicated your experiences with
> this website to others, how favorable would your
> comments be?*

When we evaluated the Net Promoter question, we found
that 40% of the survey respondents were considered Promoters, 33% were Passives, and 27% were Detractors. (Not only
were 27% Detractors, but Net Promoter also considers those
people to be a source of "bad profit.") Had we simply stopped
at this point we would have assigned a NPS score of 13%. (40%
Promoters – 27% Detractors = Net Promoter Score of 13%).

Then we evaluated results for the two additional questions
asked and found the Net Promoter metric misrepresented all
three categories by a wide margin. Worst of all, NPS overstated
Detractors by a factor of twenty-seven. The NPS question
labeled 27% of our 20,700 survey respondents as Detractors.
But only 1% of the 20,700 people surveyed said they would be
likely to communicate a bad experience.

That is what statisticians call, in technical terms, a really big
difference.

How can people who do not even talk to others about your
products or services become Detractors and the source of "bad
profits"?

In my mind, they don't.

In another study for another client we looked at so-called
"detractors" to determine if any loyal customers were found
in that bucket. We determined that while 32% were "detractors," over 60% of those so-called detractors were in fact very
loyal customers. They had paid for the service provided for at
least two years and were very likely to continue to pay for that
service in the future.

Misrepresentations of the numbers of Detractors, Passives and Promoters, if you even believe in those general categories, are caused by a basic flawed assumption—that "likelihood to recommend" can measure both positive word of mouth *and* negative word of mouth. It can't.

You simply cannot assume a person who is not likely to recommend will actively generate negative word of mouth. "Likelihood to recommend" can only measure positive word of mouth. That's why Detractors are significantly overstated using Net Promoter Score.

Then take it one step farther. If you really want to eliminate "bad profits" (I'm still trying to figure out exactly what those are), identify the people genuinely dissatisfied with your products and services and who will generate negative word of mouth as a result. Find out why using customer experience analytics, and take direct actions that will result in increased satisfaction.

And while you're at it, work hard to convert Passives into Promoters. Find concrete ways to convert good customers into long-term, loyal customers by better meeting their needs and expectations.

## Where's the Growth?

Likelihood to recommend is *correlated* with company growth and can *contribute* to future growth but in no way explains the majority of future growth and does not predict future growth. A rising Net Promoter Score does not cause revenue growth and there have been no studies that show a causal relationship between NPS and future growth. Revenue growth and a rising Net Promoter Score are correlated. On the other hand, rising customer satisfaction *causes* an increase in revenues and an increase in word of mouth recommendations. In fact, this lack of predictive ability is evidence that NPS is not an adequate proxy for satisfaction, as its creators and many proponents claim. If NPS measured satisfaction, it would predict growth (since satisfaction has been shown in numerous academic, peer-reviewed research articles to predict financial performance).

Measure NPS and you miss the point.

But don't just take my word for it. We asked economists, statisticians, researchers, professors, and PhDs to help determine whether a high Net Promoter Score leads to company growth and whether a low Net Promoter Score leads to declining revenues. Together we analyzed NPS over several years to see whether NPS was able to predict revenue growth for online retailers.

It could not. Instead we found Net Promoter Score is not a driver of growth ora measure of customer satisfaction. It accomplishes neither. It also does not help businesses decide what steps to take to improve their results.

Why?

# Insufficient Information

The rallying cry during the introduction of the Net Promoter concept was, in effect, "This is the only number you need to know." Setting aside the problems with Net Promoter Score that we have already explored in depth, is NPS really the one number you need to know? Even if it is a precise and accurate metric, is NPS the one number you would choose?

NPS is not the one number I would choose. Word of mouth is an outcome of satisfaction, but word of mouth does not explain revenue growth. If I were to pick one number, I would choose revenue... or better yet a single number that explains revenue growth. That number is customer satisfaction. (But then I would fall into the trap that the goal in management should be to only track one number.)

What can you do with one number? Measurement is critical because we cannot manage what we cannot measure. But where we really need help is in answering three questions:

1. *How am I doing?* What is my performance?

2. *Where should I focus my efforts?* Where will I get the largest return on my investment?

3. *Why should I take action?* Is the payback worth the effort?

One number can help answer the first question, but one number does little to answer the last two questions.

# The Clint Eastwood Take on Net Promoter Score

**The Good:** NPS adds focus and attention to the importance of the customer and the power of positive word of mouth.

**The Bad:** NPS wrongly assumes that people who do not recommend are "detractors" or sources of negative word of mouth and "bad profits." The value of a customer is not based on three "categories" but should be evaluated on a much more granular level. NPS fails to meet the acceptable levels of accuracy and precision that enable us to make quality business decisions.

**The Ugly:** NPS does not predict revenue growth and provides no insight into true customer loyalty.

# Simple is Just…Simple

We spent a lot of time on Net Promoter Score for a reason. NPS is a prime example of a metric that is simple to use and easy to understand but has no value as a predictive metric.

How can any result with a +/− 10-point margin of error help you make important business decisions? Would you accept that kind of margin of error from your physician?

It is impossible to convert a so-called Detractor into a Promoter when 1s are lumped in with 6s. The opinions, attitudes, and experiences are simply too different. Asking customers about their likelihood to recommend has a definite place in the Ecosystem but it is only one component in a comprehensive, interrelated customer model driven by customer satisfaction.

Predicting the future requires the use of a proven scientific methodology based on reliable metrics and an accurate understanding of the voice of customer; then you can truly manage and grow your business.

Never use metrics based on faulty math, flavors of the month, or measurement by proxy. Faulty metrics are often based on a sloppy and lazy approach to data collection, data analysis, and data integrity. Those "metrics" do more harm than good because they may cause you to make the wrong decisions for what appear to be the right reasons.

Then toss out measurements that may correlate with customer satisfaction but do not determine causal factors. Is there a link between customer recommendations and customer satisfaction? Absolutely—but instead of trying to sniff out the value of that link through inference or proxy, why not go to the source and ask the customer? Since the customer is critical to your success, shouldn't you use measurements you can count on to give you the information you need to better satisfy those customers?

Then remember counting is not measuring. It may be natural to look for proxies, because while satisfaction is a concept we all understand, "satisfaction" seems difficult to define and measure because we cannot see it.

As a result we often avoid trying to measure something that is not directly observable. Completing tasks, making purchases, abandoning shopping carts... we can count those events. All too often our Key Performance Indicators are the "things" we can count but are not the metrics that truly determine our success and growth as a business.

Until recently we could not accurately measure a concept like "customer satisfaction." Fortunately, Claes determined a methodology to accurately measure satisfaction. Over a number of years we have shown the ACSI methodology works—and we have proven that businesses benefit financially when customers are satisfied. Customer satisfaction, measured correctly, is not just credible, reliable, accurate, and precise—customer satisfaction is also predictive. I have yet to find any other customer satisfaction or customer experience measurement approach that purports to indicate satisfaction that is predictive and stands up to the scrutiny of a peer review analysis.

Finally, do not believe your own hype. Some companies embrace fuzzy methodologies like Net Promoter Score because they can use the results to try to influence Wall Street or to write glowing paragraphs in their annual reports. Those measurement efforts may provide some measure of marketing value but will never be the metrics a business can use to manage forward.

When you deploy a sound, proven methodology that measures the most important asset you have—your customers—that methodology pays tremendous dividends and helps create truly loyal customers.

# chapter 11

# EARNING TRUE LOYALTY

Our discussion of measuring customer satisfaction raises larger questions about the nature of customer loyalty.

Many people use the words "retention" and "loyalty" interchangeably. Much of the confusion surrounding customer loyalty is based on the widespread use of loyalty programs.

In business terms, I think of loyalty as a faithfulness or allegiance to a company or brand. In short, when I am loyal to a company, that company is my first choice. In broader terms there are four basic forms of customer loyalty.

## Purchased Loyalty

The best example of purchased loyalty is a customer rewards program. Other examples include memberships, coupons, and rebates. Basically, purchased loyalty pays customers to be loyal—and there is nothing wrong with that practice. In many industries and market sectors the purchased loyalty strategy works well.

The main problem with purchased loyalty is that purchased loyalty can be easily stolen. Say you set up a frequent flier account with a particular airline. If the only reason you are a loyal customer of that airline is the points system, when another airline offers a more advantageous system you will immediately switch.

Under purchased loyalty the customer is loyal to the system, not the company. Every business wants a sustainable competitive advantage. A purchased loyalty program can provide a competitive advantage, even though it may be a very tough advantage to sustain.

Purchased loyalty can also produce unintended consequences. Programs can condition customers to expect deals, discounts, and loyalty rewards. The recent growth of daily deal programs (like Groupon, Living Social, etc.) and the membership/flash sales websites (like GiltGroup, HauteLook, RueLaLa, etc.) only serves to add to consumer expectations of receiving deals or discounts.

## Convenience Loyalty

Your local market, corner dry cleaner, the coffee shop on your way to work…you might be loyal to these businesses simply because they are convenient. You are likely to remain loyal unless competitors come along who are equally or even more convenient.

Convenience loyalty can apply online as well, although less commonly. If you own the right real estate on a home page or portal you may create loyalty through convenience. But convenience advantages online are generally fleeting. The Internet has largely eliminated the power of convenience loyalty, both online and offline. "Location, location, location," is no longer the most powerful factor in retail success in today's multichannel, Accelerated Darwinism environment.

# Restricted Loyalty

Restricted loyalty exists when there is no other game in town. Your cable company may enjoy restricted loyalty, especially if you live in a rural setting and there is no competition. (Although it is easy to argue that other options do exist, like online services.)

Utilities tend to enjoy restricted loyalty. Most cities do not have multiple electricity providers. A corporate travel program with a company like American Express may be a form of restricted loyalty, especially if you feel no other programs are competitive. Arguably some Wal-Mart locations enjoy a form of restricted loyalty with a dollop of convenience loyalty mixed in. If Wal-Mart is the only game in your town, naturally you are loyal. When customers have no options loyalty is their only choice.

Constraints often create loyalty. Restricted loyalty is great for a business—if you can get it and maintain it—but restricted loyalty is increasingly a thing of the past. Competition exists in almost every consumer situation, both within an industry or category and in the larger marketplace. Companies compete, especially in down economies, for a larger share of wallet—across industries and across markets.

# True Loyalty

True loyalty is earned loyalty. True loyalty is undying allegiance to a brand or product based on an incredible level of satisfaction.

Customer satisfaction breeds true loyalty. When you are highly satisfied, when your needs are completely met and your expectations are consistently met and even exceeded, you simply cannot imagine using another product or service. True loyalty is the holy grail of customer satisfaction and is something every business should aspire to create.

In a nutshell these are the four basic types of loyalty—so what does our discussion of loyalty mean where your business is concerned?

First and foremost, the ultimate goal for almost every business is to create and foster true loyalty. When you measure the right things, listen to the voice of customer, and make changes and improvements that will cause increases in customer satisfaction, you can create truly loyal customers.

Loyal customers come back. You do not have to win them or pay to acquire and keep them. Loyal customers are more profitable as well, since new customers are much more expensive to acquire.

But in order to achieve true loyalty you must first measure loyalty.

Measuring a potential behavior such as likelihood to recommend does not measure loyalty. Likelihood to recommend measures positive word of mouth. We worked with a fantasy sports provider and found that 27% of their users said they would not be likely to recommend the provider but only 3% said they were actually likely to share that kind of feedback with others. The fact that, when asked, people said they were not likely to recommend the service did not automatically mean they would *volunteer* that information to someone else.

The key is to understand customer needs and expectations, measure results, and make changes that positively impact the customer experience and meet the real needs of customers. Along the way you may also have to purchase customers, but purchasing customers is rarely sustainable over the long term. Creating truly loyal customers by satisfying customers is a long term, sustainable advantage.

So don't be lazy. Matching a competitor's loyalty program is certainly easier than creating satisfied customers while practicing fiscal responsibility. (After all, it is easy to satisfy your customers if you don't have to be fiscally responsible. Simply spend what you want!)

Convenience loyalty is wonderful, especially if you work hard to choose the right locations or modes of delivery. Purchased loyalty has its place. Restricted loyalty is great if you can get it. But those forms of loyalty are difficult to obtain and tend to yield fleeting advantages. True loyalty based on customer satisfaction is the ultimate goal of any business and the only true, long-term competitive advantage.

How do you foster true loyalty? The process starts with understanding the elements of a useful metric.

# chapter 12

# THE ELEMENTS OF A USEFUL MEASUREMENT

**U**sefulness starts with credibility.

Every measurement or methodology must be credible. In business terms a good measurement is a measurement we can believe in and trust. The last thing any of us want to do is make a decision based on faulty logic or an imprecise, flawed system of measurement. That is why I am proud we use the American Customer Satisfaction Index as our methodology; it is the gold standard of customer satisfaction measurement.

Next, good measurements are based on principles that conform to the scientific method. (While a fascinating subject to me, I recognize the elements of experimental design are somewhat less than exciting to most people . . . so I will stay at a high level and hopefully make the topic fun.)

The next quality of a good measurement or metric is reliability. If you like, think of reliability as repeatability. Reliability is the premise that a valid experiment, repeated under the same conditions, will yield the same results time after time after time. That is why solid experimental design is so critical; the goal of a good experiment—or good measurement—is to eliminate variables so the results are repeatable and therefore reliable.

A reliable result is your friend because it helps you understand what actually happened and what is likely to happen in the future.

Reliable measurements possess two other qualities: precision and accuracy. Precision and accuracy may sound like the same thing, but they are not.

Say you're William Tell. You skip the legendary shoot the apple on your son's head trick and aim at a target instead. You shoot a total of six arrows. All fall somewhere in the center circle but hit the circle at various points of the compass. Some strike the top, some the bottom, and some the sides. You were accurate—your arrows fell relatively near the center circle every time—but you were not precise. Your arrows struck the target at different points.

Then you shoot six more arrows while your son continues to sigh with relief. Each misses the center circle completely. Every arrow strikes well to the side. But each arrow does hit a small area comprising a diameter of less than an inch. You were *precise*—all your arrows hit nearly the same spot—but you were not *accurate*. You missed what you were aiming for—the center circle—by a wide margin.

That is the difference in precision and accuracy. Any measurement you use must be both precise *and* accurate.

To extend the archery analogy further, let's bring in Robin Hood. Robin Hood attends the tournament and shoots an arrow that splits the Sheriff's arrow. He is not only accurate—he hit the center of the target—but he is also incredibly precise.

A watch provides another way to think about accuracy and precision. A watch can be accurate if it does not have a minute hand, but it cannot be precise. That watch is accurate because it can be correct. If the hour hand points to the 10, and the current time is in 10 o'clock range, the watch is accurate. But the watch is not precise. All we can know is the current time is somewhere around ten o'clock. In most situations, like timing a downhill skiing race or even getting to a meeting on time, a watch with a minute hand does not provide the precision we need. The level of precision needed is dictated by the amount of precision required to make the right decision.

We also require a valid measurement that actually measures the right things. As you know, measuring word of mouth to determine satisfaction is not a valid measurement of satisfaction and in no way measures the right things.

Sensitivity is also a critical attribute of a measurement system. While a measurement does not have to respect the feelings of other measurements, it must be able to detect change. We require a level of sensitivity that provides the intelligence to make decisions. Measuring satisfaction by a "yes" or "no" response is a far cry from providing the level of sensitivity needed to make the right decisions.

Measurement systems must have metrics that are:

**Credible**

**Reliable**

**Accurate**

**Precise**

**Valid**

**Sensitive**

The result is a measurement you can trust.

Consider our earlier discussions regarding backwards-looking and forwards-looking measurements. Accounting measurements can be credible, reliable, accurate, precise, valid, and sensitive. Financial statements can be as well.

For example, last month's gross income total—unless your culinary skills extend to cooking the books—meets the above criteria. When you follow generally accepted accounting principles and your bookkeeping procedures are sound you can rely on your gross income figures. You have both data and metrics you can trust.

Churn rate, often used to measure customer attrition, is another example of a popular business metric. To calculate churn, divide the average number of total customers by the number of customers who stop using a service. Say a company runs a membership site; its churn rate is the ratio of people who do not renew their memberships compared to the total number of average members. Since new members are often costly to acquire, maintaining a low churn rate is vital to some businesses. It is a lot less expensive and generally more profitable to keep existing members and customers than to acquire new ones. Last month's customer churn rate also meets the above measurement criteria as long as you are able to accurately collect data.

So measurements should be credible, reliable, accurate, precise, valid, and sensitive. Sounds good, right? What's missing?

Two additional attributes: predictive and actionable.

When your measurements are credible, reliable, accurate, precise, valid, and sensitive, you start from a good base. Add the ability to use measurements that allow you to take action based on your findings and predict the future and you hold the keys to long-term success.

That is where using a sound methodology to measure customer satisfaction plays its part. Using the ACSI methodology we have proven that customer satisfaction drives loyalty, retention, and word of mouth—all of which drive financial success. As satisfaction increases, sales increase. As satisfaction increases, transactions increase. As satisfaction increases, positive word of mouth increases. As satisfaction increases in one channel it drives sales in other channels. And as satisfaction increases in comparison to the competition, the likelihood to purchase increases while the likelihood of purchasing from a competitor dramatically decreases.

Customer satisfaction also predicts financial performance. Since 2000, a stock portfolio of strong customer satisfaction companies has outperformed the S&P 500 every year for twelve years in a row. (See Chapter 6, written by Claes Fornell, for more detail.) Those companies outperformed the S&P 500 in both weak and strong economies.

Customer satisfaction, measured correctly, is predictive in nature and can drive future performance.

In scientific and experiment design terms, the more closely you can measure the actual experience the better the data you gather. Great metrics should always provide powerful insight into the future intent of a customer. Great measurements help predict the future.

# The Big Three Questions

Earlier I mentioned three important questions every measurement system should help answer. The topic deserves repeating. Deploying a measurement system that is credible, reliable, accurate, precise, valid, sensitive, predictive, and actionable is the key to using analytics to manage your business forward.

Remember the big three questions:

1. *How am I doing?* What is my performance?
   **Reliable, Accurate, Precise, Valid, Sensitive**

2. *Where should I focus my efforts?* Where will I get the largest return on my investment?
   **Actionable, Predictable, Valid, Sensitive**

3. *Why should I take action?* Is the payback worth the effort?
   **Predictable, Credible, Sensitive**

An effective measurement system allows you to answer these questions with confidence—and to trust those answers and manage forward.

# Perception is Reality

Perception often drives us to take certain actions. As a result, customer satisfaction does not need to be measured exactly "on time." When you talk to customers, their perception is their reality. The perception of their last experience will determine what they do next.

But their perception will not always be identical to what actually happened.

Say you call a help center and are placed on hold. The recorded message says the wait time is ten minutes. If you reach a technician in five minutes you are happy. You are satisfied. If instead you are placed on hold and are not told the wait time, that same five minutes may seem too long to wait and you wind up dissatisfied.

The event itself, the five-minute wait, was the same in both instances. Your *perception* of the event was dramatically different based on your expectations—expectations the call center either helped or failed to create, by the way.

Another example is purchasing a product at a store. Say a product is marked with a giant "Price Reduced" sign. Your perception is you bought the product at a great price. The reality could be the price you paid was higher than you could have paid elsewhere, but nonetheless your perception remains that you paid a great price. Your perception is your reality whether that perception is accurate or not. In this case your perception determines your satisfaction, loyalty, and future behavior, not the reality of the price.

# Expectations Influence Satisfaction

Customer expectations can be established by factors like advertising, media, past use, reputation, and word of mouth.

Some expectations lie more within your control, including the way marketing messages can establish expectations before consumers interact with your brand. Once a customer is engaged, you can manage their expectations based on their actual experiences.

The quality, support, and follow-up to an experience can also influence expectations for future interactions. Customer expectations are molded and morphed with each interaction between you and your customers.

For example, our research shows customers report they are more frustrated by free shipping when free shipping comes with restrictions—especially when those restrictions come as a surprise—than they are by simply paying what they consider to be a reasonable price for shipping. If you advertise "free shipping for online purchases" and during checkout a customer realizes free shipping is offered only for purchases over $100, that customer will be dissatisfied. If the customer knows ahead of time that spending over $100 results in free shipping, their expectations are met and the odds of a satisfying experience are significantly higher.

The same is true if you promise free overnight shipping and the customer receives the package a day late. She may be upset by the delay even though originally she would have been quite happy to receive the package in three days.

In these cases *you* created an expectation—and you failed to deliver.

Here is another example. One of our clients, an apparel retailer, faced a merchandise issue that was not under the control of its web operations team. Customers repeatedly complained (through both opt-in feedback and customer satisfaction surveys) that they wanted to be able to buy accessories as well as apparel from this retailer. The corporate strategic plan did not include selling accessories online, even though those items were sold in stores and catalogs. The web operations team could not add accessories to the website so they instead posted a notice on the site:

"Accessories are not currently available for purchase on our website. We apologize for the inconvenience."

Customer satisfaction among a certain customer segment shot up immediately, not because the actual experience had been changed but because their expectations had been managed. (I must admit that is one of my favorite expectation-related stories.)

The consumer is in control, has lots of choices, and due to low switching costs is likely to go elsewhere whenever you do not meet their expectations. Meeting expectations—or failing to meet expectations—creates a perception that instantly becomes the customer's reality. Satisfaction is the combination of consumer expectation and their actual experience.

That's how you turn data into information and information into intelligence. Data is raw numbers; information is interesting and informative. Intelligence is compelling and game changing.

Even credible, reliable, accurate, and precise data is still simply data. Knowing—beyond a shadow of a doubt—that your site receives 1,000 page views per hour is hard data but it is also just information. Data is raw. Data is just a series of statements. To be useful data needs context.

Data must become intelligence.

Credible, reliable, accurate, precise, valid, and sensitive data, collected using a scientific methodology, takes key performance indicators and turns them into real intelligence that allows businesses to determine key success indicators and take specific actions that are predictive of future outcomes. Intelligence helps you manage forward instead of simply observing and reacting to the past.

# chapter 13

# TURNING INTELLIGENCE INTO ACTION

**W**e all want to drive results, build stronger companies, and benefit our shareholders, employees, and customers. To take control of your company's future:

> Measure the right things the right way

> Turn data into information and information into intelligence

> Take the right action based on good data, since gut feel takes even the smartest only so far

> Monitor results and hold yourself accountable

Accomplish these four missions and you will not just survive, you can win.

Companies that rely on analytics driven by credible, reliable, accurate, precise, valid, sensitive, predictive, and actionable metrics move from the strength of the individual to the strength of a system—and enjoy long-term success. The power of an individual only goes so far. Too many companies fail when a dynamic leader is no longer in charge. (That is one reason why many people worry about what will happen to Apple when Steve Jobs is no longer at the helm.)

Sound simple? Like many things, creating strength in a system is simple in concept but difficult to practice and execute. Measuring well is hard work.

If you do not rely on data your business is only as good as the person leading the business, which makes building long-term, sustainable success almost impossible. Great people make great decisions, but analytics-driven organizations can overcome the short- and long-term loss of key personnel. Force of personality should never rule the day, even if—especially if— you own the company.

Credible, reliable, accurate, precise, and most importantly predictive and actionable measures and methodologies must drive decisions. Give up personality-driven control and you gain even more control—and as a result you and the customer both win.

Think about it. The consumer is definitely smarter. The consumer is in control. But *we* can also be smarter, as long as we do not rely on old tactics, old strategies, and old methodologies.

Instead we all must accept that a knowledgeable, intelligent, powerful, and empowered consumer exists. Then we can pull the secret lever that drives success: Customer satisfaction. To manage forward you must understand and use the Analytics Ecosystem.

Earlier we discussed conventional metrics like time on site, page views, and other transactional measurements. Each is behavioral in nature. Behavioral data definitely has its place. Behavioral metrics like clickstream data, financial measurements, and task evaluation are a necessary and important part of a healthy measurement Ecosystem. Behavioral metrics form a set of key performance indicators to measure what happened.

Observational metrics are important. Observational metrics include session replays, usability studies, and watching users on a one-on-one basis. Observational metrics show what happened.

Feedback is helpful. Although not representative, and not a metric, all voice of customer is valuable.

Satisfaction measurements are also critical and form the most important component of the Analytics Ecosystem. Measures of satisfaction include attitudes, perceptions, and the voice of customer.

Taken together, customer satisfaction is a key success indicator. Customer satisfaction predicts what will happen in the future.

So where are the customers? Right where they belong—in the center of the ecosystem.

## The Measurement Ecosystem

The beauty of the Analytics Ecosystem is that it blends behavioral data, observation, feedback, and satisfaction with the customer—a constant and ever-present element at the center of the analytics universe. As a result "soft" is converted into science. By applying science to measuring voice of customer you can turn data into information and information into intelligence—methodology-driven, actionable, *predictive* intelligence.

Where does your business stand in terms of the Ecosystem?

Most companies fall at what we often call Level 1. Those companies use metrics and measurement tools to collect data. Level 1 is a great place to start; the fact you use metrics to generate data is a step in the right direction and is the foundation of the Ecosystem.

Companies at Level 2 use the right tools for the right purposes. They do not measure by proxy. They do not confuse opt-in feedback for a metric. They don't game the system, use faulty math or inadequate research methods, or assume simplicity equates to elegance and integrity.

Companies at Level 3 cover most of the bases by using behavioral and transactional data to start to turn information into intelligence.

Companies at Level 4 integrate the elements of the Ecosystem to not only understand and measure key performance indicators but to also determine key success indicators—and to predict what will happen. Those companies are looking and managing forward, not backwards. Managing forward allows your business to maintain a constant understanding of customer needs and expectations. Real intelligence allows your company to stay ahead of rather than behind the curve.

For example, few argue that automakers were slow to react to a rising consumer demand for fuel efficiency, and fewer still can win that argument. If automakers had maintained an effective methodology for listening to the voice of customer, they may not have needed to wait for changing consumer behaviors to a cause dramatic impact on company financials to realize that consumer demand for fuel efficiency was neither a fluke nor a short-term trend. Automakers looked backwards rather than forward—and after nearing the brink of extinction must make managing forward a key component of their business cultures in order to survive.

Focusing on key performance indicators *and* key success indicators must be an ongoing priority. Maintaining your own Analytics Ecosystem is the only way to measure results, identify causal relationships, make intelligent decisions, and predict future success.

Capturing the voice of customer is not a one-time event. Measuring customer satisfaction is not a one-time event. These must be part of the fabric of your corporate strategy.

How do you measure success? Was success yesterday? Is success today? Is success what happens tomorrow?

Real success is certainly a combination of all three, but in fact you are only as good as tomorrow. Traditional measures and accounting reports focus on the past; customer satisfaction is the future. Key performance indicators evaluate the past; key success indicators *predict* the future. Look back, look forward, and always listen to the voice of customer.

In a nutshell, that is how you Manage Forward.

Let's look at specific ways to determine and implement smart business strategies based on better knowledge of your business and your customers.

# **Managing Forward:** A Template

Every business should ask the same basic questions: How are we doing? Where should we focus our efforts to make our business more successful? Why should we take action, and is the return worth the investment?

Most experienced companies have the right ideas, but the key is to use actionable, intelligent, customer-driven data to turn those ideas into the right actions. Let's look at the process in stages.

**Stage One:** Identify Objectives and Determine the Role of Each Channel Within the Organization

Sound basic? It is—but maintaining a consistent focus on the true role of each channel is difficult. Here are two examples.

## Media

A media company is naturally made up of different channels, so understanding the role of each channel is critical in building an Analytics Ecosystem.

Start with the heritage of a newspaper company. Traditionally, a newspaper's primary channel was print, customer service was based on some form of call center, and sales were driven and managed by people.

Today the landscape is very different and much more complicated. Almost every newspaper has a website. What is the objective of the site? In reality the website serves many purposes: as a media distribution channel that will drive revenue based on ad-sales and online subscriptions, as a marketing and sales channel for traditional print and print/online subscriptions, and as a customer support channel providing a cost-effective way to provide support to millions of customers. The site has three primary objectives as well as secondary objectives like promoting investor relations, recruiting employees, etc. The addition of mobile channels requires that mobile objectives must be determined, too.

We cannot manage what we cannot measure, and we cannot measure when we do not have a defined objective.

## Multichannel Retailer

Retailers face a similar challenge: in-store sales, web sales, mobile channels, call centers...with marketing layered into the website and mobile channels. Customer service is handled across all channels. In short, multichannel retailers deploy a complex set of channels, each based on similar and different objectives.

Once we define the objectives of each channel we can define the experiences our consumers should have with each of those channels. Those definitions form the basis of your Analytics Ecosystem.

**Stage Two:** Measure Intelligently

Once again, you cannot manage what you do not measure. The core activity in this stage is to establish and implement tools and methodologies that generate credible, reliable, accurate, precise, predictive, and actionable metrics. The results create a benchmark for evaluating the results of changes and improvements and for analyzing short- and long-term trends.

Your measurement methodology must incorporate all elements of the Analytics Ecosystem in order to deliver predictive and actionable findings. Otherwise key intelligence could be overlooked or disregarded.

We recently worked with an established direct brand that enjoyed web analytic results well above industry averages. In addition, retail analysts consistently rated the company's website as the standard against which other sites should be compared. Even so, the company was concerned since their conversion rates consistently fell well below industry averages.

Since the company's main objective was to use their website to increase sales, solid web analytics results and critical praise were gratifying but largely irrelevant.

By taking the measurement process beyond behavioral data and incorporating customer satisfaction data, we were able to measure the impact of the website across offline channels; those results were higher than the company expected and accounted for some of the low conversion rate. At the same time we determined concrete steps the company could take to improve satisfaction and True Conversion rates in their online channel while improving offline sales as well.

To be effective a measurement system requires two layers of measurement:

1. **Customer Experience Level.** We must measure every experience customers have, at every touch point and transaction. By measuring these experiences through the lens of customer satisfaction and the Analytics Ecosystem we not only measure the success of each experience but also answer the Big Three Questions:

   1. *How are we doing?*

   2. *Where should we focus our improvement efforts?*

   3. *Why should we improve?*

   The answers provide the diagnostic capability to manage the *customer's experience* forward.

2. **Customer Relationship Level.** In addition to measuring each experience, we must measure the total relationship with the customer. Understanding how each experience impacts the total relationship provides the measurement intelligence to manage the *business* forward.

   A complete and properly designed measurement system provides the measurement intelligence to meet customer needs and meet and exceed customer expectations.

**Stage Three:** Set Priorities Based on Customer Satisfaction ROI

No company has unlimited resources. Understanding the needs and expectations of your customers naturally helps your business prioritize the allocation of limited resources.

The key to winning in the ultra-competitive business landscape we all face is to optimize our allocation of resources to the activities that maximize return on investment. Using a sound methodology helps us determine the impact different initiatives and improvements can make on customer satisfaction and makes prioritization much easier.

For example, a retail customer planned to spend $200,000 to improve page download times. Deeper analysis determined that increased speed, while measurable and specific, ultimately made no difference to customers. The change would generate no measurable impact on customer satisfaction or customer behavior. Our methodology showed tweaking product descriptions would have the greatest impact on turning browsers into purchasers. Making those improvements was a much more effective allocation of resources.

Until you measure intelligently you can't know the answers and cannot prioritize resources effectively. Distinctions can be subtle, though.

After analyzing the satisfaction of first-time and repeat customers, a large international media retailer found a gap in the perception of transaction costs. By testing customer price sensitivity to overall transaction costs, to product costs, and to shipping costs, they set different priorities for first-time customers and return customers and developed a pricing strategy that increased conversion rates and overall sales.

Make improvements based on applying science to the measurement of your customers. Improve your business by allocating resources to efforts that improve customer satisfaction. Then you can predictably impact customer behavior and create loyal and profitable customers.

**Stage Four:** Make the Changes that Matter Most to Your Customers

Identifying what to change is only the first step. Making changes that actually improve customer satisfaction is an all-important but often difficult task.

The Analytics Ecosystem can be of great help. Using observation to take analysis down to the individual customer level can often provide the answers.

Then make improvements, and test those improvements using the same metrics. Analyze, improve, test, analyze—keep making the changes that lead to the ROI you seek.

**Stage Five:** Benchmark Broadly

Competition does not exist solely in your category or industry. Businesses compete for a share of wallet against *all* purchases. Benchmarking performance against competitors is important, but so is benchmarking against top performers in other spaces. Learn from what makes others successful as well as from what others do wrong. (Learning from mistakes others make is a lot less painful than learning from your own.)

For example, if you sell products online you almost certainly compete not just with your direct competitors but also with companies like Amazon. Even if you do not compete with Amazon, your customers have visited the Amazon site and automatically compare the functionality and ease of use of your site against the Amazon experience. How do you compare? What should you do to match up and compete?

Benchmark against:

> Competitors

> Other industries

> Leaders across all industries

Also benchmark against your own performance over time and across multiple channels. Standardize measurement tools so you compare apples to apples, even in multiple channels— that way you can better evaluate cross-channel causal factors and the impact of initiatives in and across all channels.

**Stage Six:** Test, Test, and Test Again

Testing is a science. At its core, effective testing is based on effective measurements.

One example of testing is a usability test. Usability studies measure the user experience across key audience and customer segments. Different customers have different needs and expectations, and solid usability studies ensure those needs and expectations are assessed.

Another example is A/B testing. A/B testing compares a baseline control sample to a variety of single-variable test samples. A simple example is testing two different shopping cart systems to determine which system results in higher conversion rates and lower shopping cart abandonment rates. Another example is testing a new store layout in a select number of stores against the current store layout.

Effective A/B tests create apples to apples comparisons. The value of most channels goes beyond the transactions of that channel, so focus not only on short-term metrics like transactions and conversions but also on long-term metrics like customer satisfaction, purchase intent, and loyalty; when you do, you can truly understand the impact of site changes and determine how customers experience the changes made.

The key is to tweak changes and improvements based on test results and long-term trends. One of our clients, a national apparel retailer, determined through careful metrics monitoring that site navigation flaws created problems for users. Although metrics could diagnose the problem, metrics did not indicate how to fix the problem. (Metrics rarely indicate how to actually fix any problems.)

Our client attempted to address the navigation issue by making site architecture changes, but navigation and overall satisfaction scores declined as a result. By maintaining and evaluating the same metrics throughout the process they were quickly able to determine different—and better—ways to improve site navigation and customer satisfaction.

**Stage Seven:** Measure Success...

Customer-centric scorecards measure results both internally and in regards to your most important asset, your customers. Measuring customer satisfaction is a critical task. Higher transactions, conversions, loyalty, and profits are a by-product and result of increased customer satisfaction.

**Stage Eight:** ...And Never Stop

The bar constantly rises even as you improve your website and better satisfy your customers.

The customer has the knowledge and is in charge. On the web the punishment for failure is fast and hard. Accelerated Darwinism is survival of the fittest at a much faster rate. Measuring customer satisfaction and making predictive changes to improve customer satisfaction can never be a one-time event. The process of measurement must be continuous.

Use intelligent measurements. Turn data into information and information into intelligence. Use that intelligence to make decisions that optimize the investment. Monitor the results and link the impact of your efforts to goals like sales, conversions, retention, loyalty, and word of mouth.

And then repeat the cycle, over and over again.

In today's environment, the customer controls the relationship and can quickly and easily switch to better service, products, and value.

When we focus on satisfying the customer we reap the benefits of increased customer loyalty and customer retention—and financial success.

# chapter 14

# CUSTOMER SATISFACTION IN ACTION

The proof is in the pudding. The following brief case studies show how the ACSI methodology can be employed to measure and analyze customer satisfaction and identify specific areas of improvement. My goal is to provide a broad overview of how effectively measuring customer satisfaction, using the Analytics Ecosystem to listen to voice of customer, can make dramatic differences in any business or organization.

In some cases I will identify specific companies and organizations; in others I will simply refer to specific actions taken to improve customer satisfaction.

We will start with what might seem like an unlikely example of improvement in customer satisfaction—the federal government.

# Government Satisfaction

In 2010 the **American Customer Satisfaction E-Government Index** showed its highest overall score in six years and the largest quarter-to-quarter increase in its history.

What were the underlying factors for improvement? Let's start with a little background.

First, further analysis showed the longer a federal website had measured satisfaction, the greater the level of improvement over both the short- and long-term. (Once again, you cannot manage—much less improve—what you do not measure.) So while the Obama administration does deserve at least some of the credit for improvements in satisfaction, the fact remains that sites enjoying the largest increases have evaluated customer satisfaction—and acted on those findings—for years.

Clearly federal web managers are committed to listening to the voice of citizen. The people in charge of e-government work hard to understand what we want, need, and expect online.

The Social Security Administration website is just one example. In 2010 the Internet Social Security Benefits Application site, where citizens can apply for benefits online instead of in person at a local office, scored an 87 in customer satisfaction. (An ACSI score of 80 or higher is considered to be excellent.)

Those are outstanding results and just one of the ways we have determined citizens are more satisfied with e-government services than with traditional offline services.

The Social Security Administration should be proud of their results, but the benefits (pun intended) of citizen satisfaction extend much farther. The old joke, "If you don't like the government, it's not like you can start paying taxes to Canada," contains a kernel of truth. Dissatisfied citizens have few options, since where public services are concerned the government is the purest example of restricted loyalty. Even so, the government officials we work with display a sincere and dedicated focus on improving the satisfaction of the people they serve.

Other gains from increased satisfaction are easier to quantify. Processing benefit applications online is significantly less expensive than processing applications at a local office. Budget cuts and shrinking tax revenues, combined with a growing population that puts ever-increasing pressure on government agencies, makes cutting costs while improving customer satisfaction a win-win for officials and for citizens.

More and more of us prefer to handle certain transactions online. The easier those transactions are, and the more often our expectations for those transactions are met, the more satisfied we become—and in most cases the less expensive we become to serve.

# Amazon

Background first: holiday period research showed overall retail satisfaction scores were up compared to the previous year. The top e-retailers in particular did very well, but we saw across-the-board increases for most of the e-retailers on the **ForeSee Online Retail Satisfaction Index** while aggregate satisfaction also jumped to an all-time high.

Keep in mind the study showed many increases in satisfaction on a year-to-year basis. Previous results were terrible for many retailers, and some of the companies on the list only managed to make up earlier losses in satisfaction.

Good news, but not for everyone. The best got better while many of the rest suffered. In our weekly benchmarks that include over 110 e-retailers representing a broader spectrum of companies, scores were down consistently on a year-to-year basis.

Who was the big winner? It came as no surprise, at least to us. The gold standard of online customer satisfaction is

Amazon.com. Amazon not only achieved the highest score any company had ever received on our holiday index, but its financials backed up that result. Amazon grew revenues at a higher rate than several of the next retailers combined. Amazon sells almost everything, and as a result of outstanding customer satisfaction almost every online shopper has been to Amazon. com. Even if you do not directly compete with Amazon your customers may expect your website to provide as satisfying an experience. (If your ACSI score falls below Amazon's 87, roll up your sleeves and get to work.)

Yet Amazon was not always financially successful. In its formative years Amazon decided not to use call centers but to instead provide incredible service via email. They took returns with no questions asked. They worked hard to over-stock inventory for peak holiday periods. Over time those service strategies helped the company grow market share, loyalty, and trust.

Those service strategies were also expensive, but Amazon stayed the course and had the internal fortitude and (possibly more importantly) the capital to stick to their overall plan of *first* becoming great and *then* figuring out the economics.

Along the way there were definite missteps. A widespread customer relationship issue occurred when Amazon transitioned to selling products for other retailers. The transition was not apparent to customers; most did not realize they no longer bought directly from Amazon: you placed the order with and paid Amazon but another retailer delivered the product. The system worked fine until people had a problem or concerns. When customers needed help from a customer service representative, Amazon forwarded them to the retailer's customer service department.

Over time customers had developed the expectation of receiving Amazon-level customer service—and suddenly those expectations were not met. Customer satisfaction levels dropped.

Over time Amazon worked hard to change expectations and better support its associated retailers and their mutual customers. Based on Amazon's current customer satisfaction results the process works better than ever—but there were definite periods of declining customer satisfaction and financial struggle.

No company is perfect, but listening to customers allows a company to constantly strive to be perfect.

# Zappos

Can you take customer service too far? Companies must satisfy customers—but companies also must be fiscally responsible.

Here is a story I recently heard. A group of friends were on a trip. They wanted to order a pizza, but since they weren't in their hometown they had no idea who to call. One said, "Hey, call Zappos. They'll answer anything." They did, and the Zappos customer service rep checked an online directory and gave them the phone number for a nearby restaurant.

That is an amazing story on a number of levels. But I do wonder whether that level of service is fiscally responsible. I honestly do not know—I am not privy to Zappos operating results or financial statements.

Still, it is possible to do a great job of satisfying customers by providing outstanding customer service. Zappos realized potential customers would be hesitant to purchase shoes without first trying them on, especially if returning any shoes that did not fit resulted in additional cost to the customer. To overcome purchase hesitation Zappos offered free returns. I know people who ordered three sizes, tried them on, and returned the two pairs of shoes that didn't fit, all at zero cost—to themselves, at least.

Zappos overcame the mental hurdle of buying shoes online, albeit at great expense. Is a strategy like that fiscally responsible?

Since Amazon paid approximately $1.2 billion to acquire Zappos, the Zappos strategy is certainly hard to argue against.

But it would have been tough for me to justify, because there is definitely a point of diminishing returns on increased customer satisfaction. To restore the balance, you must know your customers *and* know your company. Be fiscally responsible while satisfying customers and you can succeed.

Now let's take a look at specific actions organizations have taken to improve operational results. While I will not identify the organizations involved, I will share specific results so you can gauge the impact of their actions.

# Drive ROI by Making Website Improvements

A major health system used ACSI-based voice of customer metrics to make its site more customer-friendly for patients, healthcare providers, and the community. By making a series of changes to its search process, like enabling site visitors to search by both common terms and by medical terms, search tools returned results visitors could better use and act upon.

Based on customer satisfaction data collected online, the health system also decided to enhance its "Find a Physician" tool, a feature used extensively by patients and health care providers.

As a result, over a three-year period the site experienced a 125% jump in visitors who searched for a doctor. More importantly, the health system enjoyed a 38% increase in online visitors who located a physician by using the "Find a Physician" tool.

Plus, as satisfaction with the web experience grew, overall site traffic also grew. In three years the total number of site visitors increased by 138%.

# Increase Profitability by Encouraging Online Self-Service

A regional energy utility website was designed to address some of the issues, concerns, and queries currently handled by a call center. ACSI-based analysis showed the utility that customers appreciated receiving general information but were much more interested in paying bills, turning service on and off, comparing energy usage over specific time periods, and enrolling in special programs offered by the utility—all online.

Once the utility introduced those enhancements to the site customer satisfaction scores soared. Higher levels of satisfaction also created a bottom line impact as the utility recognized $1.76 million in annual cost savings by reducing overall call center activity by 4%.

# Grow Revenues by Increasing Conversions

An established apparel manufacturer introduced a website designed to meet customer needs not covered in their retail network of stores. ACSI-based analysis showed the manufacturer-turned-online-retailer a more effective way to organize product lines on their website, providing the business case to upgrade product photography and product descriptions throughout the site. Once implemented, those improvements drove a 30% increase in conversions and a 100% increase in online revenues.

Guided by customer satisfaction insights, the company increased revenues from the website by 250% over the next eighteen months.

Increase Overall Satisfaction by Prioritizing Online Product Enhancements

A multichannel book retailer faced several product-related challenges on its website.

First, products were difficult to find due to an overwhelming array of available merchandise. ACSI-based customer data showed improvements to search and navigation would result in increased satisfaction and lead to an increase in desired future behaviors. The retailer made changes to the search process, including the addition of filters that enabled customers to search by criteria such as age and product price.

As a result the company saw higher overall satisfaction driven by increased scores in key satisfaction drivers. Product browsing rose by 4.5% and navigation rose by 12%. In addition, capturing customer feedback regarding items searched for but not found spurred the retailer to re-release out-of-print titles to increase sales.

# Gain Actionable Data by Integrating Customer Satisfaction with Other Web Analytics

A financial services company viewed its website as a critical tool in its focus on customer-driven innovation but lacked a scientific way to measure online success and identify improvement opportunities. By adding customer satisfaction analytics to its existing suite of web analytics, the company added the "Why?" to the "What?" to identify not just visitor behaviors but also the reasons for those behaviors. In addition, the company was able to identify what visitors were likely to do following their visits, like making a purchase offline, returning to the site, purchasing from a competitor, etc.

Linking satisfaction data to actual purchase data enabled the company to explore the root causes of satisfaction and improve the site while enhancing loyalty and purchase behavior.

# Test New Store Programs by Measuring the Impact of Programs on Satisfaction

A major women's apparel retailer planned to implement custom fitting programs in their stores. The program was rolled out to a test group of stores across the country. By segmenting and comparing stores in the test pilot program to other stores in the chain, the retailer was able to measure the execution of the rollout and the impact it would make on customer satisfaction, purchase intent, and loyalty.

Consumers who made purchases were surveyed using the ACSI methodology. Customers were asked if they had been offered a custom fitting, and if so were asked a series of additional questions about the specifics of that fitting. The retailer used the ongoing customer satisfaction measurement program to test compliance with the new program in pilot stores, creating a more cost-effective and accurate way to test for compliance than by implementing a mystery-shopping program.

The success of the program was analyzed by comparing customer satisfaction, future purchase intent, and loyalty across various segments of customers:

1. Customers in stores that were not participating in the pilot

2. Customers in stores participating in the pilot who were not offered the custom fitting

3. Customers in stores participating in the pilot who were offered the custom fitting but declined

4. Customers in stores participating in the pilot who were offered the custom fitting and accepted

The results of the analysis showed the program was a major success, increasing customer satisfaction and customer loyalty. The program was then rolled out across all stores and the ongoing measurement was used to monitor compliance and evaluate the impact of the program. The results were improved near-term financial success and improved customer loyalty.

# Gain Insight Into Call Center Effectiveness

A customer service call center is often the last opportunity a business has, from the customer's perspective, to make things right. Success at a call center can have a profound impact, sometimes transforming a disgruntled customer into a loyal customer. Failing to meet a customer's expectations at the call center can be the final push that not only drives the customer away but also possibly generates negative word of mouth.

A large call center implemented a customer satisfaction program providing agent-level satisfaction metrics. The analysis identified individual agents and teams that were underperforming compared to the rest of the organization. The analysis also identified common problems and specific issues.

The organization used the program to help build a training improvement program for call center agents that focused specifically on shortcomings identified. The organization also used the customer satisfaction program to identify the agents and teams that would benefit most from additional training. The result was greatly improved scores across call centers and individual teams, increasing customer satisfaction as well as resulting in a higher percentage of dissatisfied customers who were converted into loyal customers.

# Identify Impact of New Mobile App

A financial services company planned to roll out a mobile app to complement their website, but offering all the features on the mobile app that were available on the website would have made the app difficult to navigate.

As the rollout commenced, the company measured customer satisfaction. They evaluated how well the app met overall customer expectations and also drilled their analysis down to the feature level. Measuring the satisfaction of each feature allowed the company to identify and prioritize the features that most needed improvement.

In addition, by listening to voice of customer they learned which new features customers wanted most . Allocating resources to the functions with the biggest impact on customers led to a very effective mobile program and increased market share.

# Again: How do you turn information into intelligence?

First, get smarter. As you learn more about your customers you can step up and meet the challenge of satisfying Super Consumer. Since the consumer is in control, the importance of satisfaction is magnified—when we do not satisfy consumers they can and will go elsewhere... *fast*.

The key—which bears repeating—is to do the right things. Performance is important. Cost control is important. Key performance indicators are important. But if you only focus on key performance indicators your company can be failing and you may not even realize it.

Over the short term you can survive even if your market share is shrinking, since "all" you need to do is cut costs. (Cutting costs sounds easy on paper but is much harder in practice, of course.) Eventually, though, your company wastes away to skin and bones, with nothing left to cut...and along the way you lost all the customers you could no longer afford to service.

Take Gateway Computers. (I will intentionally simplify the tale of its demise.) Gateway, on the surface, had done everything right where customer satisfaction was concerned. Upper management showed an incredible interest in customer satisfaction levels. A key executive was responsible for customer satisfaction programs and worked hard to measure and improve satisfaction. Based on their methodology their satisfaction scores were great and bonuses were even awarded...but financial results continued to slide downward.

Worse, Gateway watched their ACSI scores decline in advance of their financial decline. (As you know, the ACSI methodology does a great job predicting financial performance based on customer satisfaction results.)

Gateway reacted quickly, replaced the entire system, and did start to turn the customer satisfaction ship—but sadly those changes were too late.

Restoring the balance can also help companies that face major competition. Few can argue that Google does not own the search business. A number of competitors have fallen by the wayside, yet some competitors have done a better job than others of holding on to their share and maintaining their position in the search marketplace.

A few years ago, one of the search providers launched a new search engine they felt would offer a significantly improved experience by providing more images in conjunction with search results. They launched the new tools and interface...and revenue numbers immediately dropped. The CEO reacted quickly. He called in the project's champion and in effect said, "Revenue is dropping. Pull it. Roll back the changes."

The project leader responded by showing how customer satisfaction levels were actually increasing as a result of the change. Customers were more satisfied by the search results, so the site was generating less revenue due to fewer page views. He predicted customers would become more loyal and generate increased revenue over the long term, and in fact that is what happened. Customer satisfaction did predict and drive customer loyalty and revenues.

Know what you know and know what you don't know. Then make sure you find out everything you can about what you don't know.

# chapter 15

# INTELLIGENCE INTO ACTION:
## MORE EXAMPLES

The right methodologies allow customer satisfaction to be measured at a high level *and* at a more granular level. We have looked at specific examples of companies and situations where understanding the customer experience with that business played (or should have played) a key role.

Customer experience analytics used within the context of the Analytics Ecosystem can also help guide companies on a broader range of issues. The following examples illustrate the possibilities. In some cases individual companies learned to manage their businesses differently. Others were guided to perform increasingly granular research on their biggest asset—their customers.

> > Free shipping. *How do retailers determine the true value of free shipping?*

> Daily deal websites like Groupon and Living Social. *Do they really generate new customers for participating businesses?*

> Social media. *How can businesses go beyond counting followers and fans and quantify the real impact of social media on the bottom line?*

> Mobile shopping. *Is mobile shopping truly prevalent?*

> Online banking in the U.K. *Can the convenience of the online channel overcome overall frustrations with banking in general?*

# Free Shipping

Many sites offer free shipping. To what end? The results of the 2010 Top 40 Online Retail Satisfaction Index show that free shipping is a valuable acquisition and retention tool for first-time visitors but has little impact on already-loyal customer decisions to purchase or recommend a website. In addition, the cost of shipping is a critical factor when a customer determines which channel to select (online or offline) and which specific retailer the customer chooses.

Clearly shipping costs impact results—both in terms of customer acquisition and in terms of profits—but what is the true cost of free shipping to an online retailer?

Using the voice of customer and the ACSI methodology, here is what we found:

**Free shipping is increasingly more common.** Approximately 70% of holiday shoppers recalled seeing some type of free shipping offer, 20% said free shipping was not offered, and the remainder were unable to remember. The number of shoppers recalling a free shipping offer continues to increase, indicating free shipping has become an ever more common business practice.

But what does that mean?

**Free shipping can be an effective conversion tool.** Customers who remember seeing a free shipping offer are more satisfied with the retailer, making them more committed to the brand, more likely to return, and more likely to purchase.

Compared to buyers who did not see a free shipping offer, consumers who did see a free shipping offer report being:

> More satisfied

> More committed to the brand

> More likely to return to the website (in general)

> More likely to return to that specific retailer the next time they seek similar merchandise

> More likely to purchase online

> More likely to recommend

> More satisfied with the retailer overall, regardless of channel

Because we measure customer satisfaction over time we are able to gain further insight. For example, we now find little difference between the satisfaction and purchase intent of shoppers who receive free shipping with and without restrictions. (A few years ago free shipping offered with restrictions resulted in lower satisfaction and likelihood to purchase, but that impact has lessened over time.)

While the root cause of this trend is difficult to determine, one assumption is that shoppers are savvy enough to work around restrictions and qualify for free shipping.

Problems still occur when restrictions come as a surprise. For example, customers who expect to receive free shipping but discover it is only available on orders over a certain dollar amount are less than thrilled; the same is true when free shipping applies to some products but not to others. If expectations for free shipping are established and clear, restrictions do not negatively impact purchase behavior as much as they once did.

**Shipping costs are a major factor in the purchase online or offline decision.** Nearly 20% of online shoppers who bought offline did so in order to avoid shipping costs—even if they researched the product online before making the purchase. Multichannel retailers who do not offer free shipping face the risk that shoppers will decide to purchase in-store from a competitor. Shipping charges should not be a major purchase decision factor; the key is to minimize the perception of shipping costs as a reason to shop offline.

| Why did you purchase in a store instead of on the website? | % of responses |
|---|---|
| Ability to receive the product immediately | 31% |
| Needed to see or feel item before purchase | 19% |
| Avoid paying shipping costs | 18% |
| Cheaper prices offline | 13% |
| Ability to talk to a salesperson | 9% |

Meanwhile, when we look at people who chose to buy online instead of offline, free shipping is not the main driver but is definitely a factor encouraging shoppers to purchase online instead of offline.

| Why did you purchase on the website instead of in a store? | % of responses |
|---|---|
| Ability to have product delivered to recipient | 50% |
| Easier/more convenient to buy online than offline | 45% |
| Ability to compare prices more easily | 41% |
| Cheaper prices than offline | 36% |
| Free shipping offer | 33% |
| Availability of customer or expert product reviews | 17% |
| Ability to redeem a gift card online | 16% |
| Product not available in store or catalog | 12% |

**Availability of free shipping is a key reason shoppers choose one retailer over another.** Free shipping heavily influenced approximately 60% of online purchasers, causing them to select one e-retailer over another. In addition, this group is more likely to purchase online in the future than online purchasers who are not particularly influenced by free shipping.

What do these results this mean for e-retailers? Shipping costs matter to shoppers. High shipping costs—or the perception of high shipping costs—drives customers to buy in stores. Low shipping costs drive online purchases. Not only do shipping costs influence the purchase channel but they also influence the choice of retailer.

Understanding customer behavior helps businesses understand the true cost of free shipping: on customer satisfaction, sales, and overall results.

# Groupon and Living Social: Should You or Shouldn't You?

As this book is written, widespread speculation regards the sustainability of Groupon's business model as the company prepares to go public.

In a study conducted in spring of 2011 of the top 100 online retailers we explored the daily deal phenomenon more closely. We found that Groupon and Living Social do bring in new customers, welcome news to businesses and daily deal companies alike.

The following background data provides context to our findings.

**Approximately two-thirds of Top 100 site visitors are enrolled in at least one Daily Deal email program.** Over 14,000 of the more than 22,000 respondents we surveyed who visited the top 100 retail websites are enrolled in at least one program. Groupon is the most popular site among those who subscribe to daily deals; it has approximately twice the number of subscribers as its closest competitor, Living Social, and more than twice the number of purchasers.

Although competitors appear to be slowly catching up, as of this writing Groupon is solidly in the lead in this space.

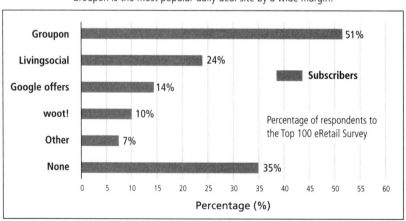

**About Two-Thirds of Top 100 Site Visitors Are Enrolled in At Least On Daily Deal Email Program**

Groupon is the most popular daily deal site by a wide margin.

*Source:* ForeSee Spring 2011 Top 100 E-Retail Satisfaction Index

Of those who subscribe to daily deals, 46% subscribe to more than one service, a number that should continue to rise. Put another way, simply because some Living Social and Google offers have gained traction does not necessarily mean Groupon will lose subscribers. The result could be a market where there is enough pie for everyone (of course the pies are sold at half price!)

**Not only do shoppers subscribe to daily deals, they use them.** This is good news for consumers, retailers, and the sustainability of the daily deal business model in general.

Nearly two-thirds of subscribers to daily deal programs purchased at least one deal in the past ninety days, regardless of which site they subscribed to, and 89% of those buyers redeemed one or more offers during that period.

| Most people who buy offers use them. | %* |
|---|---|
| I have used more than one offer in the past 90 days | 55% |
| I used one offer | 33% |
| I have not used any offers yet | 11% |

* percent of visitors to Top 100 retail websites who purchased offers.
Source: ForeSee Spring 2011 Top 100 E-Retail Satisfaction Index

Now for the most interesting and relevant discussion regarding the future of the daily deal business model and the individual companies in the space:

Do Groupon and Living Social actually help companies to acquire new business, or do they simply allow existing customers to receive better deals on products or services they would have purchased at or near full price?

That is the million-dollar question. Sadly, there is good news and bad news.

**Daily deals do bring in new business...but also give deals to frequent customers.** Of the people buying daily deals, 38% were already frequent customers of those businesses. Existing customers, even loyal customers, received significant discounts to purchase what they would likely have purchased without a daily deal. The added value of a daily deal is minimal at best, eroding margins and potentially turning loyal customers into discount seekers.

On the positive side, 31% of daily deals represented new business made up of customers who were not aware of or who had limited brand exposure to the company. (27% were infrequent customers and 4% were former customers.)

As a result, at least 35% and arguably 62% of deal buyers represent *new* business. This is compelling data regarding the type of customer the daily deal model is intended to generate—new customers.

Once acquired, it is up to you to meet their needs and satisfy them. In fact, it is up to you to not only satisfy new customers but to satisfy them to the level that allows you to convert a percentage of new customers into loyal, long-term customers.

**Daily Deals Do Bring in New Business**

Who buys daily deals?

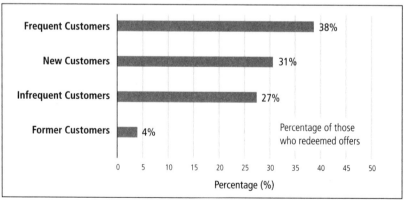

*Source:* ForeSee Spring 2011 Top 100 E-Retail Satisfaction Index

Many businesses use daily deals, from retailers and salons, to bowling alleys and dentists, those businesses will inevitably experience different results. Still, customer experience research can at times provide guidance, especially if that guidance is specific to your business and your customers.

Would a daily deal like Groupon cost your business money or generate higher profits? The key is to ask your customers about likely future behaviors and make decisions regarding the use of daily deals based on their answers.

# Social Media: What is the Value?

I am asked this question by Chief Marketing Officers fairly often. While there are great tools that can monitor and measure activity on social networks, understanding the value of that activity is another matter entirely.

How do you quantify the contribution of social media marketing to your bottom line? Are your social media initiatives driving purchases or future behaviors like offline purchases or the use of your website as a primary resource?

Questions like these drove us to create the Social Media Value Calculation, a measure of the degree of influence social media initiatives have on the consumers' decision to visit a website, store, or call center. Businesses can gain greater insight into how much their social media efforts impact acquisition by linking social media influence with the conversion activities they track. This connection ties social media marketing directly to conversions/transactions and, if applicable, to dollar amounts so return on investment can be calculated.

Here are some interesting findings from our March 2011 Social Media Value Calculation benchmark, a study that included 188 websites (in industries across the board) and more than 295,000 customer responses.

Here is what we found:

> Only 1% of site visitors came directly from a social media network via a referring URL

> Yet 18% of site visitors were *influenced* by social media

For the retailers in the benchmark (as opposed to the many non-retail companies still tracking social media value), we found that shoppers influenced by social media had a higher average order size than those not influenced to visit by social media.

That finding could indicate social media drives a higher *quality* of traffic, regardless of quantity.

Additional social media research we have conducted shows that when customers rate their satisfaction with various retail touch points, they are actually more satisfied with their interactions on Facebook and Twitter than many other channels, including retailer websites. In general, this could indicate retailers do a good job using social channels to satisfy customers.

**Satisfaction Comparison: Retail Touchpoints**

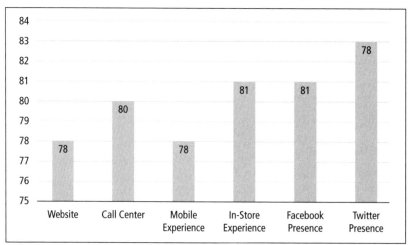

*Source:* ForeSee Spring 2011 Top 100 E-Retail Satisfaction Index

What social sites are most e-retail shoppers using? No surprise here. Facebook.

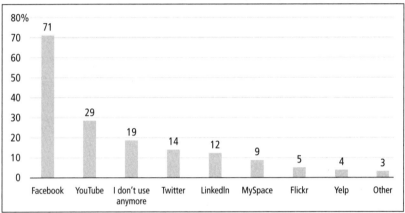

**Which of the following social media
website do you use regularly?**

*Source:* ForeSee Spring 2011 Top 100 E-Retail Satisfaction Index

But where do they want to hear from retailers? 42% don't want to hear from retailers at all on social sites.

**Which social media website would be your first choice
for receiving communications from this company?**

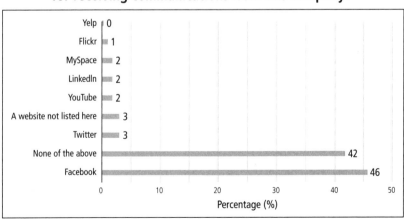

*Source:* ForeSee Spring 2011 Top 100 E-Retail Satisfaction Index

42% of survey respondents say they do not want to interact with retailers on social sites, but the next question indicates that only 29% actually do not interact with any retailers, indicating some people who *say* they do not want to interact with retailers on Facebook already do. (That is why it is important to always use a methodology that digs deeper.)

In fact, 69% of online shoppers interact with at least one retailer on social networks. Social media can be a huge growth area for retailers; as consumers start to make purchases on Facebook and other social sites, understanding how that experience impacts first-time and loyal customers will be critical.

| How many retailers do you interact with on social sites? | % of respondents |
|---|---|
| 1 to 5 | 37% |
| None | 29% |
| 6 to 10 | 17% |
| 11 to 20 | 8% |
| More than 20 | 7% |
| Don't know/not sure | 2% |

*Source:* ForeSee Spring 2011 Top 100 E-Retail Satisfaction Index

Understanding why your customers come to your site can help identify useful content on social pages. Most people choose to friend, follow, or "like" a retailer on a social site to learn about sales, special offers, and products. Very few do so for customer support.

We also see that more than half of those who interact with a retailer on a social site have made a purchase because of that interaction. This is a real testament to the power of the offers posted on Facebook and Twitter.

| Why do you interact with this company on social media sites? | %* of respondents |
|---|---|
| Learn about sales/special offers | 51% |
| Learn about products | 42% |
| Another reason | 4% |
| Get customer support | 3% |

| Have you ever made a purchase as a result of this company's sales/special offers you learned about through social media? | %* of respondents |
|---|---|
| Yes | 56% |
| No | 40% |
| Don't know | 5% |

| Have you acted on this company's sales/special offers you learned about through social media (Please select all that apply) | %* of respondents |
|---|---|
| Yes, I investigated the company's offer (clicked on a link, visited a website, etc.) | 61% |
| Yes, I shared the offer information with others (sent an email, posted it on another site, tweeted about it, etc.) | 33% |
| No, I have not acted on this company's special offers through social media | 17% |
| Don't know | 4% |

*Source:* ForeSee Spring 2011 Top 100 E-Retail Satisfaction Index

Here is a final point regarding the value of social media. We consistently ask about customer acquisition sources, and there have been a few major shifts between 2010 and 2011:

> Internet advertising and traditional media are both significantly down as a driver of website traffic

> Social media, along with email marketing, are both significantly up as drivers

> Company familiarity is also up (which could be due to more exposures/touch points on social media)

| Which of the following most influenced your recent decision to visit this company's website? | 2011 | 2010 | % Change |
|---|---|---|---|
| Advertising on social networks | 3% | 2% | 56% |
| Familiarity with site/company/brand | 36% | 30% | 18% |
| Instant Message from a friend or colleague | 1% | NM | NA |
| Internet advertising | 3% | 14% | –77% |
| Internet blogs or discussion forums | 4% | 1% | 163% |
| Link from a shopping comparison website | 2% | 2% | –29% |
| Message directly from the company on a social network | 2% | NM | NA |
| Message or recommendation from a friend on a social network | 6% | 1% | 331% |
| Mobile phone text messages or alerts | 1% | 0% | 109% |
| Product review website(s) (CNET, Epinions) | 2% | 2% | 4% |
| Promotional e-mail(s) from the company | 17% | 12% | 47% |
| Search engine results | 9% | 10% | –10% |
| TV, radio, newspaper, or magazine advertising | 6% | 12% | -51% |
| Video I saw on YouTube | 3% | NM | NA |
| Word of mouth/recommendation | 7% | 8% | –8% |
| Couldn't find what I was looking for in stores/catalogs | NM | 3% | NA |
| Had a gift card I wanted to redeem | NM | 3% | NA |

Source: ForeSee Spring 2011 Top 100 E-Retail Satisfaction Index

How customers use social media—in general and to interact with businesses—will continue to evolve. The key is to determine how *your* customers use—and *want* to use—social media to interact with your brand.

# Mobile Shopping: How Prevalent?

Like social media, mobile is a touch point with enormous potential. When customers rate their satisfaction with various touch points, their satisfaction with mobile is relatively low compared to other touch points (although it is on par with overall website satisfaction.) These findings are not likely to be the case for long.

Here is the chart shown earlier:

**Satisfaction Comparison: Retail Touchpoints**

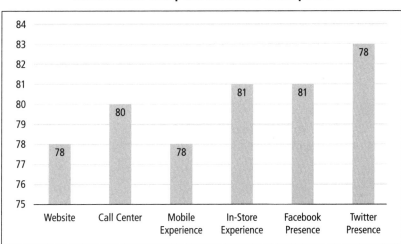

*Source:* ForeSee Spring 2011 Top 100 E-Retail Satisfaction Index

As you know, from the customer's point of view satisfaction can be defined as how what you received compares to what you expected to receive.

The average consumer may not currently understand that mobile websites and mobile apps are fundamentally different than regular websites. More and more, consumers expect the same functionality and the same navigability between mobile and web experiences. Yet very few retailers deliver fantastic mobile experiences. The technology is simply too new.

Here are three strategies to manage customer expectations that will certainly see increasing use over the coming year:

1. Improve mobile sites and apps

2. Adjust customer expectations

3. Apply a combination of the two

Let's take a look at how many online shoppers use their phone to visit a retailer, whether through a regular website viewed on their mobile phone, through a mobile-optimized website, or by using an app.

How many? Very few report using their phone to visit a retailer. That finding is likely to change dramatically in the next year, though.

**Have you ever accessed this retailers's website, mobile website, or mobile app from a mobile phone?**

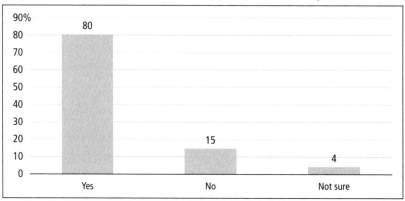

Source: ForeSee Spring 2011 Top 100 E-Retail Satisfaction Index

Most people look for price or product information in some manner, and 17% actually plan to purchase using a mobile phone, a percentage will only continue to grow.

| How did you visit this retailers mobile website or mobile app? | % of respondents |
|---|---|
| To look up price information about a product | 51% |
| To compare different products | 43% |
| To look up product specifications | 31% |
| To view product reviews | 25% |
| To make a purchase | 17% |
| To find a store location | 11% |
| Another reason | 6% |

*Source:* ForeSee Spring 2011 Top 100 E-Retail Satisfaction Index

Different retailers will obviously experience different results; that is why understanding what your customers arrive for can help you design mobile offerings with the customer in mind.

Everyone in our industry talks about mobile. For many years we have anticipated the "Year of Mobile." Possibly 2012 will be that year.

# Online Banking in the UK: Surprisingly High Satisfaction

We have researched customer satisfaction with online banking in the U.S. since 2003, and this year we conducted our first studies on satisfaction with online banking in the United Kingdom.

For the 2011 UK Online Banking Study, we conducted more than 1,000 customer surveys of customers of the top five consumer-oriented retail banks: RBS, Lloyds, Barclays, HSBC, and Santander.

Despite over two years of tumult in the global banking industry, customer satisfaction with online banking in the UK is fairly high and customers are very satisfied with the top five banks. (On aggregate they score an 80, generally considered the threshold for excellence on the study's 100-point scale.)

Within the top five banks, the range of scores varied from 77 to 82, indicating close competition between the top banks.

The results were, quite frankly, surprising. How can customer satisfaction be so high when so many banks and financial markets are in trouble?

The answer lies in the online channel. Banking websites have an amazing ability to connect with and satisfy customers. Customers can have a satisfying and fulfilling online banking experience despite conditions in the financial markets. That is great news for banks—a channel works, and works well.

That is also great news for companies who may suffer from shifts in public opinion, national disasters, or other crises.

We cannot compare satisfaction year-over-year in the UK (at least not yet), but we can compare between the U.S. and the UK. In other industries we study (like retail), there are much larger gaps in satisfaction between the U.S. and UK markets, but in online banking, the gap is only three points (when we compare customer satisfaction with the top five UK banks to an aggregate of satisfaction with all U.S. banks).

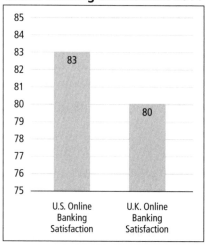

**Country Comparison:**
**Online Banking Satisfaction 2011**

*Source:* ForeSee Spring 2011 Online Banking Survey

Another way to provide context to is to compare online industries. The next chart shows how satisfaction with online banking compares to satisfaction with online retail in the UK. There is quite a gap, and where satisfaction is higher, financial returns are higher.

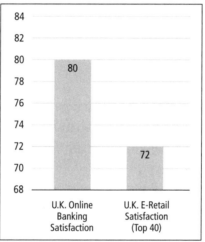

**UK: Online Banking vs. E-Retail Satisfaction**

*Source:* ForeSee Spring 2011 Online Banking Survey

Other key findings from our UK research:

> **Adoption of mobile banking is slow.** Of survey respondents with a mobile phone, only 15% are aware of mobile banking apps or mobile sites for their bank (by my current count, only two of the top five banks in the UK even *have* a mobile site—Barclays and HSBC— and even those do not appear to have apps.) The other three banks (Santander, RBS, and Lloyds) do not have a mobile site or apps. Whatever the reason, only 10% of respondents use their mobile phone for banking.

> **UK customers prefer to hear from their bank through the post (or as we say in the U.**S., snail mail). When asked their preference for communications from their bank, 42% said they prefer post, 38% prefer email, 11% prefer the website, 3% want text messages or mobile alerts, and only 5% said they want no communications at all.

> **UK customers are not inclined to get "social" with their bank.** When asked if they would like to friend, follow, or "like" their bank on social media sites like Facebook, 97% said no.

> **There is a clear relationship between satisfaction and frequency of website usage.** Customers who access their banking website roughly once a month have a satisfaction score of 71, while customers who access their banking website more than once a day have a satisfaction score of 89.

> **UK customers prefer the website to other channels by a huge margin.** When asked which channel they are most satisfied with, 70% said the website. 17% said the branch, 10% said the cash point, two percent said the call center, and one percent said mobile banking.

Customer experience-based findings like these can provide broad guidance to banks—or at least encourage them to ask their customers what they need, expect, and want. In fact, all of this research, from Groupon to social value to mobile, can help companies struggling to develop and implement customer-focused strategies.

Better yet, companies can perform their own research about their customers. After all, every company's customers differ quite a bit, even when customer demographics and offered services are nearly identical. Every company-customer relationship is the result of a complex and broad set of factors that can and should be taken into account when a company works hard to manage their business forward.

Understanding customer behavior helps businesses understand the true costs and benefits of various investments in terms of customer satisfaction, in terms of sales, and in terms of overall results.

# chapter 16

# MANAGING FORWARD

**H**ow do you manage your business today?

Managing your business with an analytics-driven approach is a good start, but it takes more than that. Most people manage their business by looking backwards. Knowing what has happened in the past helps but is not enough. "What worked before should work again," can often seem a safe assumption. But the world today (consumers, competitors, and technology) moves at a fast pace. No longer can we rely only on the past to give us the direction we need.

We can gather significant data about our business and our customers. We can assemble numerous metrics and KPIs. Many dashboards are available.

Most look backwards. We have all heard the saying, "Past performance is no guarantee of future results." That is true, not only regarding our investment portfolios but also our businesses.

The competition is fiercer today than ever. Consumers have the knowledge and the ability to choose competitors and channels. Switching costs are lower than they have ever been. The consumer is in control. Never before has satisfying the customer been more important than it is today.

Satisfying your customers starts with understanding your customers. But satisfaction is more than just a voice of customer program. Satisfaction is applying science to the often-fuzzy voice of customer. The methodology of The American Customer Satisfaction Index allows us to apply science to the voice of customer. When we use a proven, credible, methodology that has the reliability, accuracy, and precision we need, when we use a methodology that is predictive and provides actionable intelligence, we gain the competitive advantage needed to not only survive these competitive times but to thrive.

Tom Davenport wrote a great book, *Competing on Analytics*. Now we must take the next step and compete and *win* on forward-looking customer analytics.

Managing forward is taking the next step, moving from an analytics driven company to a forward-looking analytics company. Managing forward is using customer analytics to help drive your resource allocation decisions. Managing forward is using the methodology of The American Customer Satisfaction Index to know how you are performing, where you should apply your resources, and why you should apply those resources. Managing forward is staying one step ahead of your competitors.

Managing forward with the right analytics can give you a competitive advantage.

It takes only two things to be successful in business today. Be fiscally responsible, and satisfy your customers. Those goals are not easy things to accomplish, but if we can we will be successful.

I think of managing forward as one way to quantify the value of customers as an asset. Customers are a company's greatest asset, and the best managers seek to protect company assets and achieve returns on those assets.

Consider managing forward as a compass that directs the course of your company. Most companies are shaped by financial constraints, strategic issues, entrenched corporate cultures, mergers and acquisitions...the list goes on and on. Those factors are indeed a daily reality and must certainly play a role in driving tactical and strategic decisions.

Present and future customers also drive smart, successful companies. Making the customer a key component in your strategic navigation system allows you to truly drive your company—because then you take care of the most important asset on your balance sheet.

Of course everyone says something to the effect of, "It's all about the customer," or, "The customer is Job One." Chances are every CEO references customers in his or her annual reports. Sadly, in most cases most companies only pay lip service to customers. If the only real way your leader utilizes customer satisfaction data is to add pseudo-statistical weight to press releases and reports, those metrics and methodologies are a gimmick.

Then you do yourself, your company, and your customers a huge disservice.

In the Ecosystem, customers and by extension potential customers are a key driver of the way you make decisions. Understanding the importance of the customer is not just a flashy insight; understanding the importance of the customer foreshadows great financial news because the customer is the path forward. Hit a home run with your customers and you create loyalty, retention, great word of mouth...and you gain and maintain a competitive advantage by using customer satisfaction in your corporate navigation system.

Winning through customer satisfaction is based on restoring the balance by making intelligence actionable. Balance means returning the company-customer relationship to something approaching the equilibrium of knowledge.

Currently your customers are in control. Your customers now know a lot about you...so how do you shift the balance back so you know a lot about the customer?

Remember, the goal is not to wrestle control back from customers—far from it. Some may wish they could, but there is no need to take power away from the customer. An empowered customer can actually be your company's best friend—empowered customers are *free* to choose you.

Instead, empower your company to satisfy your customers and better meet their needs.

How?

Become more knowledgeable about your customers. Know what they know. Know their intentions. Know their expectations. Know what satisfies them. Know, understand, and act upon what drives their behavior. When you become more knowledgeable about your customers, you do not simply create a competitive advantage.

You know your customers. The key is to learn even more about your customers, turning customer intelligence into a science. No longer is it acceptable to base decisions on opinions, to think, to feel...you absolutely must turn data into information and information into intelligence. And while you're at it, monitor results and link those results to conversion, retention, loyalty and word of mouth goals.

Sound like a lot?

It is easier than you think. And it works—in the public and private sector.

A few months ago, I spoke at a government conference. During the lunch break I sat down at a crowded table and introduced myself. I recognized one of our customers. We spoke briefly and, as I always do, I asked if we were doing a good job for his organization.

He narrowed his eyes, reached for his briefcase, and slammed a report down on the table.

I tried to maintain my composure, especially since the sound of the binder hitting the table attracted a lot of attention...but inside I was more than a little alarmed. I like to think I have a great handle on how our customers feel about our efforts, but still....

"This is the report you deliver to me every month," he said. "I have to tell you," he continued, "every month I have vendors coming to tell me they know what's right for our citizens.

"I tell them," he said, pausing for a beat before continuing, "I *already* know what's right for our citizens. *This* report tells me what's right for our citizens."

I have told that story a few times and people are sometimes surprised to learn a government agency cares deeply about customer satisfaction. But many e-government leaders do—and they have the results to show for it. So do companies in a wide variety of industries and sectors.

You can give your customers more. When you give your customers more, you begin to create true customer loyalty built on a solid base of customer satisfaction. Before you know it, customers will start to market for you, without being asked, and in a powerful way.

Who gets it? Who uses customer satisfaction to their advantage? One example is Best Buy.

Consumer electronics is an incredibly tough industry. The landscape is littered with failures and bankruptcies. Best Buy is arguably the only national consumer electronics company that still survives. In a challenging marketplace filled with online competitors, Best Buy optimizes its value by focusing on its customers. Sure, they make mistakes—we all do. But by keeping the focus on the customer they continue to thrive where others have not.

Best Buy is not alone in facing major challenges. Forget for a moment the impact of the global economy. The reality is that most companies have lost the power over the customer they once enjoyed in quasi-monopolistic situations. Accelerated Darwinism and Web 2.0 (is Web 3.0 on the way?) are here to stay. Customers are not only more knowledgeable, they have too many choices and virtually no switching costs.

Harsh reality? Hardly. By focusing on the customer as a predictive guide, we can restore a measure of balance to the company-consumer balance and predict what actions we should take to maintain that balance—allowing companies and consumers to benefit as a result.

Here is another example. Ask many companies why they first built their websites. Some will say it was the lure of selling products; others simply felt they needed a web presence for marketing purposes. (And many still view their websites that way.)

Smart companies understand customers make decisions based on a variety of different intentions. Not every customer visits your site with the intent of making a purchase. No matter how hard you try or how clever your site design, you will not convert them all.

Recognizing and acting on disparate intentions actually provides lasting opportunities to create satisfied customers. Provide the information a potential customer needs and you satisfy that customer. Meet a customer's needs when they want a replacement part and you create satisfaction and build loyalty. Fix a problem and you satisfy that customer—and sometimes generate more loyalty than if they had never had a problem at all.

Most people use the Internet to search for information. And where else can you provide better information and service—at a lower cost—than on the web? Where else can you so readily make investments that improve service and lower costs?

If you maintain a significant online presence, my guess is your marketing department currently runs your website. But customer service also has a role to play. The Internet can allow you to provide better service while lowering your cost of providing that service—and allow you to easily handle occasional spikes in service demand.

Let marketing continue to play a role in your website, but think of "return on customer" as more than just a sales or revenue proposition. Think about the customer, all day every day, and let customer satisfaction guide your actions.

If you do, trust me. The rest will work itself out.

One of my favorite examples of return on customer is DTE Energy, a Michigan-based company providing gas and electric utility services to over three million Michigan homes and businesses as well as energy-related services to companies across the country. DTE operates in a tough environment, an industry experiencing deregulation and an ever-present need to increase market share to enable economies of scale, but by focusing on better ways to service and satisfy customers they have generated millions of dollars in savings.

Like the Social Security Administration, DTE understands the importance of voice of customer—and embraces the customer's role in driving revenue and success. Utilities understand the importance of Return on Customer...the government understands the importance of listening to its citizens...so I feel sure you understand just how important your customers really are.

Here's another example that is more personal. Years ago Dell was justifiably praised for creating satisfied customers. I was a believer too. For years I bought computers from Dell; I didn't think twice when I needed a new computer.

But over time Dell failed to listen to the changing needs of their customers. They focused primarily on operational strategies like their incredibly efficient build-to-order process. Along the way they outsourced customer service functions to India, primarily for economic reasons. Customer satisfaction began to drop—for a variety of reasons—and the build-to-order model became less relevant as consumer needs changed.

The last time I bought a Dell laptop I realized I was frustrated by a process I once enjoyed. It took twenty minutes to "build" my system online and then I was forced to wait three weeks for the laptop to be delivered. Dell's original competitive advantages— product innovation and the ability to purchase a computer with the exact components individual customers wanted—were no longer nearly as important, to me or to most customers.

I don't need a customized laptop. Most people don't need a customized laptop. Dell did not lose me as a loyal customer because they failed to innovate. They lost me because the process of purchasing a computer went mainstream. Today I can walk into any Best Buy and choose between twenty or thirty different laptops—and take one home with me.

Dell was also late to the multichannel opportunity. In its early days, Dell maintained a competitive advantage simply because they did not incur the cost of a bricks-and-mortar presence. They discarded the traditional retail sales paradigm and built a new business model based on online sales and build-to-order. Today build-to-order no longer meets the evolving needs of customers. And in the meantime, Dell's offline retail strategy is at best a token effort. Go to Best Buy and you may see two or three Dell models at most.

What happened? Does build-to-order continue to meet customer needs? Is build-to-order important in today's marketplace? Are Dell's multichannel distribution efforts working if they are at best a token effort? The computer industry has done a great job segmenting the market. Some buyers want systems perfect for gaming, others need productivity tools, and others just want to conveniently access the Internet. In a segmented market, building systems to meet specific needs is relatively easy. Custom building is less relevant and the process can actually be frustrating for customers. Too many choices can actually make the process difficult and reduce overall customer satisfaction. ("Do I really have to go through all this just to buy a computer?")

Aside from product design, the main drivers in the computer business are service and delivery speed. Progress made in the online retail world has changed consumer expectations forever. In most cases when I hit the "Complete Purchase" link on a website my order will be shipped in a day or two. That is now my expectation.

I am no longer happy or even remotely satisfied when my computer takes three weeks to ship.

My needs and expectations have changed. I have evolved. Customer needs and expectations have changed, too.

Dell is now changing, working to catch up with what their customers need, want, and expect.

You and I now live in a world of Accelerated Darwinism.

Let's embrace the challenge of the consumer revolution. In the process we can treat customers better, help our economies function more efficiently, and create better life experiences for everyone around us. When we make the right decisions we are successful, and that success is not just limited to our companies and our shareholders. Meeting the needs and expectations of our customers helps everyone live happier, more satisfied lives.

Your customers have high expectations—and they should. With the right data, the right information, and the right intelligence, we can meet those expectations.

We can manage forward. We will manage forward.

We must manage forward.